404

Essential Tests
for
IELTS

General Training Module

By Donna Scovell, Vickie Pastellas & Max Knobel

Adams & Austen Press – Sydney, Australia

Acknowledgements

The authors and publisher are grateful for permission to use copyright material. We would like to acknowledge the original sources of text material listed below. Permission has been sought to reproduce all material whose source could be identified. Information that will enable the publishers to rectify any error or omission in subsequent editions will be welcome.

We'd also like to thank UCLES for permission to reprint the IELTS bandscales and to reference material from 'The IELTS Handbook' accessible online at:

http://www.ielts.org

The authors used the names of real organisations and drew on published articles to create the texts, but facts have been changed so that the finished piece permits inferences to be drawn and questions framed to suit the fundamental purpose of this book (which is to give an understanding of the IELTS testing process).

The facts set out as content in this text should not be relied on or quoted for any purpose except in the context of this book. The passages have been written with the express purpose of providing strategic guidelines for teachers and students in preparation for the IELTS test.

Practice Test 2 Reading Part 1 Passage 1 was adapted from a segment on Channel 7's "Creek to Coast" program shown on 26 July 2003.

Permission has been granted by:

– Aequus Partners (*http://www.workplaceflexibility.com.au*) to use and adapt the information in Practice Test 1 Reading Part 2 Passage 2

– Tourism New South Wales (*http://www.visitnsw.com.au*) to reproduce the information in Practice Test 2 Reading Part 1 Passage 2

– Murdoch University (*http://osh.murdoch.edu.au*) to use and adapt the information in Practice Test 2 Reading Part 2 Passage 1

– BayROC (*http://www.bayarearecycling.org*) to use and adapt the information in Practice Test 3 Reading Part 2 Passage 1.

Illustrations by Max Knobel, cover design by Roman Balla (rballa@bigpond.net.au), recording produced by Peter Whitford with assistance from International Casting Service, Sydney.

Special Thanks to

The authors would like to thank Christabel Lee, Jan Snowball and Terry Peck for their help in reviewing and/or trialling the materials used in these tests. We would also like to thank our colleagues and friends who supported us throughout the process of writing these tests.

Published in Sydney, Australia 2010

Updated regularly

ISBN 978-0-9751832-4-3

Adams & Austen Press Pty. Ltd. A.B.N. 96 087 873 943
PO Box 509, Marrickville, New South Wales, Australia 1475
Tel: 612-9590-4469   Fax: 612-9590-4471
Email: aap@aapress.com.au   www.aapress.com.au

About the Authors

The authors have more than 40 years of combined experience teaching English to overseas students across a variety of sectors. In addition to teaching and preparing students for the IELTS test, much of their experience has revolved around writing programs for academic English and university preparation courses.

By the Authors

'404 Essential Tests for IELTS – Academic Module' International Edition:

Book:	ISBN 978-0-9751832-0-5
Cassettes(2):	ISBN 978-0-9751832-1-2*
Book & Audio CDs(2):	ISBN 978-0-9751832-2-9
Study Guide CD-ROM:	ISBN 978-0-9751832-8-1**

'404 Essential Tests for IELTS – General Training Module' International Edition:

Book:	ISBN 978-0-9751832-3-6
Cassettes(2):	ISBN 978-0-9751832-1-2*
Book & Audio CDs(2):	ISBN 978-0-9751832-4-3
Study Guide CD-ROM:	ISBN 978-0-9751832-9-8**

* the listening test is the same for both Modules of the test
** Multimedia CD-ROM – video, audio and practice tests

Published by Adams & Austen Press

'101 Helpful Hints for IELTS – Academic Module' International Edition:

Book:	ISBN 978-0-9587604-6-1
Cassette:	ISBN 978-0-9578980-0-4*
Book & Audio CD(1):	ISBN 978-0-9578980-6-6

'101 Helpful Hints for IELTS – General Training Module' International Edition:

Book:	ISBN 978-0-9587604-9-2
Cassette:	ISBN 978-0-9578980-0-4*
Book & Audio CD(1):	ISBN 978-0-9578980-9-7

'202 Useful Exercises for IELTS – International Edition'

Book:	ISBN 978-0-9587604-7-8
Cassette:	ISBN 978-0-9578980-1-1
Book & Audio CDs(2):	ISBN 978-0-9578980-7-3

'202 Useful Exercises for IELTS – Australasian Edition'

Book:	ISBN 978-0-9587604-5-4
Cassette:	ISBN 978-0-9578980-2-8
Book & Audio CDs(2):	ISBN 978-0-9578980-5-9

* the listening test is the same for both Modules of the test

English Test Vocabulary Kit

'Activating 1001 Academic Words for IELTS'
– a unique method for all English test candidates
Book and Multimedia CD: ISBN 978-0-9578980-3-5

Online IELTS Course

'101 Helpful Hints Interactive Online Course for IELTS'

http://ielts101.aapress.com.au

FOREWORD

When Donna, Vickie and Max approached Adams & Austen Press with a manuscript that promised four complete practice tests for IELTS, we were initially cautious. Perhaps every teacher has a book inside them, and many have tried to write short tests at some time, but not everyone can write tests that are more than a superficial attempt at cloning a test such as IELTS.

Would these tests be, then, a mere presentation of a number of typical IELTS question types – as so many IELTS books on the market seem content to be these days? From the outset, our IELTS range of books has attempted to go much further than this, advising students what to do in no uncertain terms in order that they might improve; and not provide just another opportunity to 'take a test'.

It was, then, with pleasure and some relief that we sat down to discover a solid book of, yes, four complete and thoroughly trialled tests, with questions chosen judiciously and with a great deal of thought as to what was being tested – as is the case with the official IELTS tests. It was immediately apparent that the test material on offer was rigorously engaging, thought-provoking and entertaining at one and the same time.

Accompanying this work were two manuscripts for in-depth Study Guides to further unlock the secrets inside the tests.

In a word, the tests and the books were essential.

The 404 Essential Tests for IELTS.

Terry Peck

UPDATES

Please check online for updates to this book and others in the IELTS series at:

http://www.aapress.com.au/updates/

CONTENTS

INTRODUCTION

CONTENTS continued

THE FOUR PRACTICE TESTS

APPENDICES

INTRODUCTION

Do you want to immigrate to, study at school or undertake work experience in an English-speaking country?

Studying abroad at English-speaking universities and tertiary institutions has become a growth industry. This has made the idea of living or working abroad a real alternative as well. Many more people than ever before, from countries all over the world, are moving to live, work or study in English-speaking countries.

This book is designed to help prepare those who wish to immigrate, work or study in such situations.

What is IELTS?

The International English Language Testing System – or as it is commonly referred to, the IELTS test – is one of the few tests which governments, employers and educational institutions accept as being able to determine English language proficiency.

IELTS tests the four macro skills of listening, reading, writing and speaking. Students who wish to do undergraduate or postgraduate study in an English-speaking country need to sit for the *Academic Module* of the IELTS test. This means that the reading and writing sections of the test are focused on academic topics and educational settings. A *General Training Module* of the IELTS test is given to would-be immigrants, workers or students at non-tertiary institutions. The context of this module is broader and it includes more social, everyday situations in the reading and writing sections.

The two modules share the same listening and speaking tests. The differences are in the reading and writing tests. The two test results are not interchangeable, and it is important that you do the correct module for your circumstances. If tertiary education is your goal, you should plan to sit for the Academic Module of the IELTS test. If you are unsure, you should check with the organisation, immigration consultant or institution that you are dealing with.

Like any test, there are skills that you can learn and practise in order to achieve the best possible result. Being prepared for the IELTS test can make a difference to your result. For each of the four different sections of the IELTS test, a score is given from 0–9. These band scores are interpreted as follows:

Score	Description	Detailed description
9	**Expert User**	Has fully operational command of the language: appropriate, accurate and fluent with complete understanding.
8	**Very Good User**	Has fully operational command of the language with only occasional unsystematic inaccuracies and inappropriacies. Misunderstandings may occur in unfamiliar situations. Handles complex detailed argumentation well.
7	**Good User**	Has operational command of the language, though with occasional inaccuracies, inappropriacies and misunderstandings in some situations. Generally handles complex language well and understands detailed reasoning.
6	**Competent User**	Has generally effective command of the language despite some inaccuracies, inappropriacies and misunderstandings. Can use and understand fairly complex language, particularly in familiar situations.
5	**Modest User**	Has partial command of the language, coping with overall meaning in most situations, though is likely to make many mistakes. Should be able to handle basic communication in own field.
4	**Limited User**	Basic competence is limited to familiar situations. Has frequent problems in understanding and expression. Is not able to use complex language.
3	**Extremely Limited User**	Conveys and understands only general meaning in very familiar situations. Frequent breakdowns in communication occur.
2	**Intermittent User**	No real communication is possible except for the most basic information using isolated words or short formulae in familiar situations and to meet immediate needs. Has great difficulty understanding spoken and written English.
1	**Non User**	Essentially has no ability to use the language beyond possibly a few isolated words.
0	**Did Not Attempt The Test**	No assessable information provided.

(Source: http://www.ielts.org)

In this *404 Essential Tests for IELTS* the focus is on the General Training Module and four complete tests are provided.

It may help candidates to have a certain level of general knowledge before going into the test, but the test itself does not require any specialized vocabulary or technical expertise. The correct answers can be found within the confines of the test and it is advisable for any student planning to take the test, to learn the skills needed to find the answers.

After taking the test, candidates will usually receive their results in around two weeks. Test results are generally valid for two years.

- Your results will show a score for each section of the test as well as an overall score. You can now get a half band score (4.5, 5.5 etc.) for all the different test sections: Listening, Reading, Writing and Speaking.

- You cannot pass or fail this test – you are always given a score. Whether this score is high enough depends on what you want to do. Check to see what score you need for your situation.

If you don't get the required score in IELTS the first time, from May 2006 you no longer have to wait three months to retake the exam. However, it is recommended that you study hard for at least 10 to 12 weeks before re-enrolling to take the test again.

How can this book help?

1. It introduces you to the *different sections* of the IELTS General Training Module.
2. It familiarizes you with the *instructions, language and question-types* used in the IELTS tests.
3. It improves your English level by introducing you to *new language structures* and reinforcing what you already know.
4. It provides you with *four complete practice tests,* which should be taken under test conditions, and answers to those tests. A *Study Guide to the 404 Essential Tests for IELTS* is also available for you to contemplate the reasons why you got any answers wrong in these tests.

Candidates who plan to take the IELTS Academic Module should work through the practice tests in *404 Essential Tests for IELTS – Academic Module.*

If you are determined to succeed, you will need to:

1. read and practise the GENERAL POINTERS.
2. ensure that all practice tests are done under exam conditions.
3. familiarise yourself with the test format.
4. immerse yourself in English as much as possible, particularly as you approach the exam date.

Some of the skills and language taught in different sections of this book will be referred to in other areas. For example, often the topics that are used in the reading and writing sections of the test are similar. Linking words (discourse markers) too, are not only useful in making a piece of writing more interesting, they can assist in finding an answer in the reading passages and help you to tune into an answer in the listening test.

What about the future?

As candidates, you will have many reasons for taking the General Training Module of the IELTS test. Whether your plan is to work in an international company, work or study in an English-speaking country, or immigrate on a more permanent basis, the skills you learn here will broaden your knowledge of the English language. The 101...404 IELTS range will provide you with tips and hints that increase your competence in English and help you to achieve your related goals.

TEST DESCRIPTION – LISTENING SECTION

You will be presented with four different listening passages with a variety of question types to answer.

LIMITS *Approximately 30 minutes*
Unlike the reading test, you will get extra time at the end to transfer your answers to the Answer Sheet.

There are FOUR distinct sections of 40 questions in total.
You will hear each section ONCE only.
Each listening is more difficult than the one preceding it.

Section 1	Section 2	Section 3	Section 4
Usually a conversation between two people. Sometimes a third person might be involved or introduced to the conversation. Usually in two parts. Can be a social or an academic setting.	Usually a monologue of a social / functional nature. For example, an outing, a tour guide giving instructions or directions. Can be a social or academic setting.	Usually a conversation between two to four people. For example, a dialogue between two students regarding a tutorial, an assignment or oral presentation to be given. Usually in an academic setting.	Usually a lecture or speech given as a monologue. Sometimes the person is introduced by a second person at the beginning or a few questions might be asked during the course of the lecture. In an academic setting.
About 4 minutes listening time	About 3 – 4 minutes listening time	About 4 minutes listening time	At least 4 – 5 minutes listening time

A monologue = one person speaking
A dialogue (a conversation) = two or more people discussing a topic

The sections may be divided into two or more distinct parts. There may also be a pause in some of the sections to give you time to look at the questions relating to that part of the test.

It is important to note that poor spelling and incorrect grammar will be penalized, so you should check carefully after transferring your answers to the Answer Sheet.

POSSIBLE TOPIC AREAS:

Most of the IELTS listening tests are about social and educational situations. Often they are in an academic context set on a university campus discussing student orientation programs (introductions for new students to courses or institutions), details of assignments, classes or tutorials or plans for excursions, holidays or outings. The discussions might be between two students; a professor or lecturer and a student; or an administrator and a student.

The topics are usually of interest to students in their late teens or early twenties. There are information-giving and information-sharing situations.

As with the other sections of the IELTS test, you do not need to have any specialist knowledge to do well in the listening test.

GENERAL POINTERS:
- *Become familiar with the instructions used to introduce the sections.*
- *Read questions carefully and try to anticipate what you might hear.*
- *Use a highlighter pen to highlight key words.*
- *Think about and listen out for other forms of the key words and synonyms.*
- *Learn to identify question types.*
- *Know your numbers and figures!*
- *Keep looking ahead to the next two questions, so you know where you are in the listening passage.*
- *Don't be distracted by anyone or anything – concentrate!*

GENERAL LISTENING ADVICE

Do	Don't
Read the questions before the start of each section and highlight key words.	Don't panic if you miss an answer.
Listen out for linking words and discourse markers to help you follow what is happening.	Don't guess any answers unless you cannot find the answer or evidence for an answer and your time is almost up.
Check your spelling and grammar. Does the word you have chosen fit grammatically, and should it be singular or plural?	Don't listen for enjoyment – your purpose is to answer the questions only.
Look for synonyms of key words in questions.	Don't worry if you can't understand or hear every word. Remember that the rhythm of spoken English means that the most important words are always stressed the most. Learn to listen for those.
Guess – if you cannot find the answer.	
Transfer answers quickly but carefully.	Don't leave any spaces on your Answer Sheet – you don't lose marks for wrong answers.

WORDS / TOPICS / PHRASES OFTEN USED IN LISTENING QUESTIONS:

The words and topics listed here are not restricted to particular sections of the listening test.

Section 2	Section 2	Section 3	Section 4
Personal Details	**Information Giving**	**Information Sharing**	**Information Giving**
number sequences	money, prices	drafts	lecture
phone and fax numbers	dates	plagiarism	I'd like to begin with
addresses	giving directions	seminar	...which leads me to...
postcodes	maps	tutorials	in other words
dates	before that	tutor	What I mean by that is
opening and closing times	plus	lecture	To sum up
family name	refundable deposit	lecturer	study guide
first name	non-refundable	textbooks	orientation
4 in the morning till 6 tonight	altogether	resource	series of lectures
decimal pont	includes the $4 each way single (ticket)	research	due to
percentage %	£10 return (trip)	extension	outline
Celsius °C	cents	due date	
Fahrenheit °F	pence		
degrees	the high street		
double 6 (66)	the main street in the town		
triple 7 (777)	for up to two weeks		
fractions ¼ ½			
registration			
student number			

QUESTION TYPES:

The IELTS listening tests use a variety of question types which are described in the table below.

Type of question	Example of direction given on tape	Skills needed	Test strategies
Multiple choice	*In Questions 1 – 5, circle the correct answer.*	Identifying types of answers expected – what, why, when, etc. Listening for specific information.	Highlight key words in questions. Identify answers that seem unlikely & then find proof before eliminating them.
Short-answer questions	*Answer Questions 1 – 5.*	Listening for specific information. Identifying parts of speech used and required.	Highlight key words. Listen for specific words but also ideas – paraphrase.
Completing sentences, tables, flow-charts, forms, summaries, etc.	*Complete Questions 1 – 5 by using **NO MORE THAN THREE WORDS**.* *Complete the following table according to...* *Fill in the gaps...* *Mark on the map...*	Distinguishing between examples and main ideas. Identifying parts of speech. Identifying discourse markers and signposting (words that show you what part the speaker is on – e.g. First, next, then etc.) Identifying headings and main ideas.	Contractions are not used when word-limits are given. Don't use more than the number of words allotted. Look at given information to identify the type of information required. Scan given notes in summaries to frame your own note-taking.
Labelling diagrams	*Listen to the directions and choose the appropriate letter.* *Label the diagram by writing...*	Understanding relationships between words (discourse markers). Sequencing and following chronological order. Listening for specific information.	Brainstorm any vocabulary or knowledge that you have of the picture or topic.
Classifying	*Study the table and place the articles in the correct column.* *Write A for Always, N for Never and R for Rarely.*	Understanding the relationship between words. Listening for specific information. Distinguishing examples from main ideas.	Use a highlighter to separate different characteristics of categories. Use given information to determine relationships if necessary.
Matching lists, phrases or pictures	*Choose the picture which best shows...* *Match the places with the...*	Listening for specific information. Understanding cause and effect.	Identify the most obvious answers but then find proof before selecting them.

IMMERSION IDEAS:

1. Make sure you know <u>how words sound</u> – say unfamiliar words aloud, don't just read them silently.

2. Listen to as much English as possible – listen to different accents including British English on the BBC, Australian English on the ABC and American English on Voice of America, watch DVDs in English.

3. Use some of the following websites to listen to English:

   www.bbc.co.uk/worldservice/index.shtml
   www.esl-lab.com   www.cnn.com   www.abc.net.au

TEST DESCRIPTION – READING SECTION

The IELTS General Training Module Reading Test is very different from the Academic Module Reading Test. This is one of the reasons why the scores for the two modules are not interchangeable.

LIMITS *60 minutes including transfer of answers to a separate Answer Sheet*

There are three parts with 40 questions in total.
Parts 1 and 2 usually have two sections with reading passages in each of them.
Each section will contain between 750 to 900 words.
Each passage is more difficult than the one preceding it.
The question types within each passage become progressively more difficult.

Part	Detailed Description
1	The reading passages in this part use social English found in everyday situations in an English-speaking country. The passages may be instructions, advertisements, and notices. They are designed to test the candidate's ability to extract and understand information.
2	The reading passages in Part 2 use English in a language-training context. As such, they are often situated in a language school or college.
3	Part 3 has one longer reading passage. It is similar to the passages found in the Academic Module Reading Test, but it is likely to be more of a description than an argument.

GENERAL POINTERS:
- *Never read any text before looking at the related questions.*
- *Use titles, headings, underlined or highlighted words and diagrams as part of your scanning process.*
- *Read the first and last sentences in each paragraph to locate topic sentences.*
- *Learn to identify question types.*
- *Think about synonyms, paraphrases and modal verbs.*
- *Remember the time-limit – 15 minutes per text should be your goal.*
- *Buy a highlighter pen and use it!*

It is difficult to predict the content of the General Training reading passages in the IELTS test. The topics covered in the reading sections can be related to educational contexts, social activities or general knowledge. It is difficult, then, to prepare and practise vocabulary lists for any specific topic as the potential range and level is very wide. However, it is always a good idea in your test preparation work to develop and maintain effective strategies for vocabulary learning. You should develop a system of recognising new vocabulary and recording it in a meaningful way that makes sense to you. Many students like to write the word or phrase in English, record which part of speech it is, write a translation or the meaning in English, and then use the vocabulary in a sentence that makes the meaning clear.

The following format can be used by students in a vocabulary notebook:

Word or Phrase	Translation / Meaning	Sentence
enhance (verb)	To improve in value or quality	The company is keen to make a good impression and thereby enhance their reputation abroad.

You need to make sure you set yourself daily goals with respect to identifying, learning and using that vocabulary. Remember that the IELTS test does not require you to have any specialist knowledge prior to taking the test and that the answers will therefore be in the texts themselves. It will be a great deal easier to find those answers if you have practised a sound vocabulary learning technique!

GENERAL READING ADVICE

Do	Don't
Read the questions before reading the passage.	Don't start reading without knowing <u>why</u> you are reading.
Check if there is a glossary – use diagrams, highlighted words, titles and headings to help you get a general idea of the text.	Don't guess any answers unless you cannot find the answer or evidence for an answer and your time is almost up.
Be conscious of discourse markers to establish relationships between words, sentences and paragraphs.	Don't read for enjoyment – your purpose is to answer the questions only.
Use context clues and word-building skills to understand difficult words.	Don't deviate from your exam time plan.
Look for synonyms in the reading passage of key words in questions.	Don't worry about unknown words unless they are necessary.
Guess if you cannot find the answer.	Don't leave any spaces on your Answer Sheet – you don't lose marks for wrong answers.
Think about which type of answers can be guessed very quickly if you are short of time (True/False and multiple choice, for example).	
Transfer answers quickly but carefully.	

SUGGESTED EXAM TIMEPLAN FOR READING SECTION:

You have 60 minutes to complete the reading section of the IELTS test. You must transfer your answers to the answer sheet provided WITHIN THAT TIME.

0:00	Begin Part 1 – start by checking if there are two or three reading passages in the section. Allocate your time accordingly. Then, before starting each set of questions, glance at the title, diagrams, pictures, headings, etc. Then read the questions and answer as many as possible.
0:15	Guess remainder of questions that relate to Part 1 but put a question-mark beside these to remind yourself later that you have guessed these answers.
0:16	Begin Part 2 – read the questions and answer as many as possible.
0:31	Guess remainder of questions that relate to Part 2 but again, put a question-mark beside these to remind yourself later.
0:32	Begin Part 3 – read the questions and answer as many as possible.
0:50	Guess remainder of questions that relate to Part 3.
0:51	Go back to Part 1 – try answering the guessed questions.
0:53	Go back to Part 2 – try answering the guessed questions.
0:55	Transfer all questions carefully but quickly to the Answer Sheet.
0:58	Use the remaining time to double-check any answers to the last few questions in Part 3 that you guessed earlier.

Remember that each passage is more difficult than the preceding one.

Allow 15 minutes each for Parts 1 and 2 but give yourself 18 minutes to complete Part 3.

Remember however, that you will have time to go back and check on your guesses at the end of the test – do not spend time checking your answers or changing your answers.

Practise all tests using this formula.

QUESTION TYPES:

A variety of question types is used in the reading passages and you need to be familiar with techniques used in each. If any other question type is used, the test will include an example – however, this is unusual.

Type of question	Example of direction used	Skills needed	Test strategies
Multiple choice	*Choose the correct letter from A – D and write it in boxes 6 – 10 on your Answer Sheet.* OR *Choose **TWO** letters from A – D. Write your answers in boxes 1 and 2 on your Answer Sheet.* Where there are two answers for one question: *Choose **TWO** letters from A – D. Write your answers in box 5 on your Answer Sheet.*	Skimming for general impression or gist Scanning for specific (usually factual) information Understanding the relationships between words and paragraphs (discourse markers)	Highlight key words. Eliminate other answers.
Short-answer questions	*Answer the questions below using **NO MORE THAN THREE WORDS** for each answer. Write your answers in boxes 1 – 3 on your Answer Sheet.*	Scanning for specific information	Use techniques to find answers to who, what, when, where questions. Highlight key words in questions and look for these key words or synonyms in the passage.
Choosing from a heading bank	*The text above has 5 paragraphs A – E. Choose the correct heading for each paragraph/section from the list of headings below. Write the correct number I – VIII in boxes 1 – 5 on your Answer Sheet.*	Skimming for general impression or gist Identifying main ideas in paragraphs Locating topic sentences	Always read headings first and then topic sentences (or first sentence in paragraphs). Do not read whole paragraph. Do not complete in order given. Choose the most obvious answer first. Roman numerals are often used: I, II, III, IV, V etc.
Matching lists and phrases	*Look at the following people (Questions 1 – 4) and the list of opinions below. Match each person with their opinion. Write the correct letter A – F in boxes 1 – 4 on your Answer Sheet.*	Understanding relationships between words and paragraphs (discourse markers) Paraphrasing and synonyms	Choose the most obvious answers first.

Table continues on the next page...

QUESTION TYPES continued:

Type of question	Example of direction used	Skills needed	Test strategies
Identifying viewpoints, facts and opinions	Do the following statements agree with the information given in the text? Write: **TRUE** if the statement agrees with the information, **FALSE** if the statement contradicts the information, **NOT GIVEN** if there is no information on this. Do the following statements agree with the views of / summarise the opinions of / reflect the claims of the writer in the passage? Write: **YES** if the statement agrees with the views of the writer, **NO** if the statement contradicts the views of the writer, **NOT GIVEN** if it is impossible to say what the writer thinks about this. Write your answers in boxes 1 – 3 on your Answer Sheet.	Recognising opinions and viewpoints Recognising main ideas Interpreting information Making inferences	Look at the language used in the passage – is it negative or positive when discussing the topic? Is it emotional or factual / technical? Be careful of questions that use broad statements like all, always. Make sure that you know the differences in meanings of modal verbs.

Classifying	Classify the following animals as
	  A mammals.
	  B reptiles.
	  C birds.
	Write the correct letter from A – D in boxes 1 – 6 on your Answer Sheet.
		Scanning for information
		
		Understanding relationships between words and passages (discourse markers)
		
		Paraphrasing and synonyms
			Use a highlighter to identify the character of different categories in the text.

Completing sentences, tables, summaries, etc.	Complete each sentence with the correct ending A – G from the box below. OR Complete the summary / notes / table below using words from the box. OR When the test does not provide a bank of possible answers: Complete the notes / table / summary / below. Choose **NO MORE THAN THREE WORDS** from the passage for each answer. Write your answers in boxes 1 – 3 on your Answer Sheet.	Scanning for information Summarising Identifying parts of speech Paraphrasing Sequencing	Contractions are not used when word limits are given. Don't use more than the number of words allotted. Check the question to see if it asks for your own words or words from the text. For summaries and clozes, make sure that you have a general understanding of the passage before starting to complete. Information in summaries and clozes is usually in the same order as the passage.

IMMERSION IDEAS:

1. Read as much English as possible – buy magazines such as "National Geographic", "Newsweek" and "Time"; become aware of current social issues and discuss them in English with your friends.

2. Buy English newspapers.

3. Borrow a couple of English science textbooks and try following some process descriptions. This will also help your Task 1 writing.

4. Use some of the following websites to see what's current:

    www.ap.com   www.reuters.com   www.news.com.au
    www.cnn.com   www.bbc.co.uk

TEST DESCRIPTION – WRITING SECTION

The writing section of the IELTS test General Training Module consists of two tasks – both requiring different skills.

Task 1: Writing a letter addressing a particular issue. You may have to explain a situation, take steps to address a problem, or ask for information based on the facts given. In completing the task, you will have to be ready to write about wants, needs, likes and dislikes, and also to be able to express your opinion.

> **LIMITS** *20 minutes (recommended only)*
> *Minimum 150 words (no maximum limit)*

Task 2: Expressing and justifying your opinion; making an argument for and/or against a particular topic; and also outlining a problem and suggesting solutions. You may also have to clearly describe a situation, as well as challenge ideas or evidence, using the correct language and structures for both.

> **LIMITS** *40 minutes (recommended only)*
> *Minimum 250 words (no maximum limit)*

The two writing tasks in the IELTS test are different in many ways and as such should be prepared for and practised for differently. The Study Guide for *404 Essential Tests for IELTS* looks at the steps involved in the writing process for both tasks using concrete examples and sample answers. It includes guidelines that IELTS candidates can use to frame answers in suitable structures.

POSSIBLE TOPIC AREAS & QUESTION TYPES:

Task 1:

The topic areas for the Task 1 writing are of general interest, so it is virtually impossible to study all of the possible topics for this part of the test. Topics can cover areas as widespread as travel, health, leisure activities, safety issues, education, shopping, and day-to-day life issues.

Candidates should be:

- familiar with the structure of a personal and business letter.
- able to use standard phrases that commonly appear in letters, such as

    Yours sincerely,   **Yours faithfully,**   **Regards,**   **Dear Sir,**   **Dear Madam,**

- able to easily recognize the type of letter they need to write. For example, this could be a letter of request, a letter of complaint or a letter providing information.
- able to write in an informal, semi-formal or formal register (manner) and recognize which is appropriate according to the question.

WORDS OFTEN USED IN WRITING TASK 1 QUESTIONS:

apologise / give an apology
explain / give an explanation
suggest / make a suggestion
enquire / make an enquiry
complain / make a complaint
inform / provide or offer information
ask for something / make a request
describe / give a description
give details
give/provide reasons

WRITING TASK 1 – SAMPLE QUESTION

You should spend about 20 minutes on this task.

> *You recently bought an item of clothing from a shop. You discovered that it had a fault and returned it to the shop for replacement or refund. However, the assistant told you that this was against the store's policy.*
>
> *Write a letter to the store manager. In your letter*
> - *explain the problems you have had*
> - *ask for a refund or exchange on the item.*

Write at least 150 words.

You do **NOT** need to write any addresses.

Begin your letter as follows:

Dear Sir or Madam,

WRITING TASK 1 – SAMPLE ANSWER

As a general guide, the letter should be structured in the following manner:

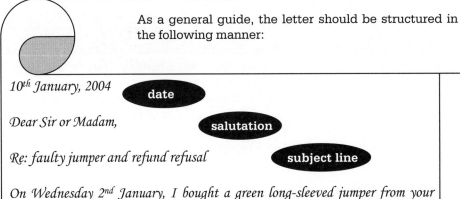

10ᵗʰ January, 2004 — date

Dear Sir or Madam, — salutation

Re: faulty jumper and refund refusal — subject line

Body of the letter

On Wednesday 2ⁿᵈ January, I bought a green long-sleeved jumper from your store. The jumper was medium-sized and made from cotton. It cost $59.95 and it was not on special.

When I got home, I discovered that there was a small hole in the left sleeve. It looks like a rip of some kind and the stitching has unravelled. I returned to your shop the next day to ask for an identical replacement jumper. Unfortunately there were none in stock. Therefore I asked for a refund. However, the shop assistant refused to give me a refund because it was not the policy of the store.

I am writing to demand a refund or, at the very least, a replacement jumper – the jumper is unwearable as it is and I do not want to buy anything else. I hope that you can assist me in this matter. If I do not get satisfaction, I will be forced to seek legal advice.

Yours sincerely, — complimentary close

S. Milne — signature

Susan Milne. — name

POSSIBLE TOPIC AREAS & QUESTION TYPES:

Task 2:

As with the Task 1 letter, the topics for the Task 2 are of general interest and so it is almost impossible to study all of the topics for this part of the test specifically. Topic areas can range from health, leisure and social issues, to education, the physical environment and travel. It is always helpful, however, to try to keep up-to-date with social issues and current affairs as this kind of knowledge is useful when writing, and indeed when doing any part of the IELTS test. Discussing issues with friends and forming opinions about things will also help candidates to express their thoughts adequately within the time limit.

Candidates must produce a certain style of writing to suit the task in question. This may include one of the following:

- **argument** – where you might need to give your opinion, or agree/disagree with a statement
- **description** – where you need to describe a situation clearly and appropriately.

WORDS OFTEN USED IN WRITING TASK 2 QUESTIONS:

describe	give reasons and make suggestions
discuss	give reasons and suggest solutions
evaluate	compare and contrast…
(critically) analyse	*"To what extent…?"*
provide arguments for and against…	*"To what degree…?"*
provide reasons why…	*"How far…?"*

ASSESSMENT:

Knowing how your writing is assessed will help you to improve your writing skills for the IELTS test.

Skills tested in both Tasks 1 and 2

- Spelling and punctuation should be of a reasonable standard.
- The register, style and content should be appropriate and relevant for the task.
- Grammar and sentence structure should show variety and maturity.
- The question should be analysed and answered correctly – make sure you actually answer the question and don't write anything that is not relevant.

Additional skills tested in Task 1

The following will be tested. The student's ability to:

- present information in a well-organised easy to follow way
- include appropriate content: use relevant and appropriate information and ideas in the letter
- organize the information and ideas into the correct style and register – that is, use a letter format and either a formal, semi-formal or informal style.
- use correct vocabulary, language and structures appropriate for the task.

Additional skills tested in Task 2

The following will be tested. The student's ability to:

- use appropriate vocabulary, language and structures.
- use appropriate content and ideas.
- present opinions in a logical, clear way.
- justify an opinion and give appropriate examples.
- agree or disagree with a statement and give appropriate explanations.
- use appropriate content and ideas.
- use correct vocabulary, language and structures appropriate for the task.

GENERAL WRITING ADVICE

Do	Don't
Be mindful of the time limits.	Don't use a dictionary when you practise your writing, as you can't take one into the exam.
Read the question carefully and then check that you have answered the question correctly.	Don't spend too long on Task 1. You need to allocate about 20 minutes to that. After that time, go on to Task 2.
Take time to plan the things you are going to write. You need arguments and examples to support your ideas.	Don't use the same vocabulary all the time.
Think about using linking and sequencing words to help your writing to sound more cohesive.	Don't use the same sentence structure and linking words. Show your knowledge by using variety and complexity.

GENERAL POINTERS:
- *Learn to interpret questions and identify question types and writing styles.*
- *Practise and rewrite corrected essays.*
- *Decide which task you will do first and make this decision long before the test date.*
- *It is important to understand that your writing cannot improve without much practice.*

IMMERSION IDEAS:

1. Do at least one piece of writing per week in examination-mode – start immediately and use the practice exercises given in *202 Useful Exercises for IELTS*.

   Always be mindful of the time limits.

   Don't use a dictionary as you practise your writing – you can't use one in the test.

2. Become knowledgeable about current affairs and social issues because you might be able to use some of these ideas in your writing – particularly in Task 2.

   Discuss them in English with friends and build your vocabulary in this area.

3. For Task 1, familiarise yourself with the format of a personal letter and the language appropriate for different registers.

4. For Task 2, familiarise yourself with different sentence structures; the passive voice; and words (in particular, verbs and adverbs) that will aid you in completing the task.

TEST DESCRIPTION – SPEAKING SECTION

Many students find this part of the IELTS test the most daunting because it happens face-to-face with the examiner – there is no hiding. However, it shouldn't be an unpleasant experience and there are many opportunities to help yourself. For instance, you should be aware that you can ask for a question to be repeated. The interview is the shortest of the four tests and most candidates cannot believe how quickly the time goes. The one thing that you have to remember is that it is a speaking test – if you don't speak and make a deliberate attempt to show the examiner your ability, then the examiner has no choice but to give you a low mark. Most examiners want to give you a good score, but they will not do so unless you communicate effectively with them.

LIMITS *Total interview time is from 11 – 14 minutes*
3 parts in total

Part 1	Part 2	Part 3
Introduction / general questions about yourself	**Long turn**	**Two-way discussion between you and the examiner**
The examiner wants to get to know who you are and what you like doing. He / she will also try to relax you so that you don't feel too nervous.	The examiner will give you a card with details of a particular topic. He / she will give you about a minute to prepare for your long turn to speak.	The examiner will ask you more difficult questions related to the topic in Part 2. The questions are designed to test your speaking level.
Relax – answer the questions in full sentences.	Take your time and speak clearly and sensibly.	Answer the questions as best you can.
About 4 – 5 minutes	About 3 – 4 minutes which includes preparation time	About 4 – 5 minutes

POSSIBLE TOPIC AREAS:

Part 1 topics are usually general in nature – asking about you, your family, your interests, what you do, your study and what your future plans are. It is an introduction, so consider the type of things that an English-speaking person might ask when they first meet you. Speak clearly.

Part 2 topics might focus on such topics as:

- a particular person such as a teacher you had in school, a famous person or a sporting celebrity,
- a particular event like the Olympics or the start of the millennium,
- a place that you have visited etc.

There are prompts on the card to help you structure your long turn, so make sure that you use these prompts wisely. Don't ignore them.

Part 3 is designed to test your speaking ability. The examiner will ask you questions that give you the opportunity to exhibit your range of vocabulary and grammatical structures. Answer the questions as fully as possible and if you don't understand a question, ask for it to be repeated.

QUESTION TYPES:

It is impossible to tell you the precise questions that will be asked in the Speaking Test but if you consider the type of speech functions that are being tested, you can prepare yourself more adequately.

In the IELTS speaking interview, you should be prepared to

- give information (personal and non-personal)
- give your opinion and justify it
- explain and/or suggest something
- express your preference for something
- compare and/or contrast something
- summarise and analyse
- describe something or narrate an event
- speculate
- check on comprehension
- repair, maintain and extend a conversation.

Impressing the examiner and increasing your band score:

It is possible to achieve an IELTS band score of 5 or above, if you have an intermediate level of English. (5 is often the minimum required for speaking for entry to any tertiary program.) A candidate who achieves Band 5 is described as a Modest User "… coping with overall meaning in most situations", still "… likely to make many mistakes" but "… able to handle basic communication in own field".

Before undertaking an IELTS test, ask yourself if you can

- communicate effectively in English with your peers.
- use some complex grammatical structures accurately e.g. all basic tenses, all conditionals (except perhaps 3rd conditional), the passive voice.
- insert discourse markers and linking words into your conversation.
- manage to express most ideas without having to get new vocabulary from the dictionary.
- make complex sentences that explain and extend your ideas.
- understand a variety of English accents (e.g. British, Australian, American, New Zealand, Canadian).
- use appropriate conversational and cultural interaction in a variety of situations.

Answering yes to all of these points, means that you have the ability to score a minimum 5 in IELTS, if your performance in each of the three parts of the interview demonstrates this ability.

In order to improve your result, you must demonstrate the ability to carry out all of the speech functions listed above, without making systematic technical errors – that is, grammar, vocabulary or (sentence) structure errors that occur repeatedly. Systematic errors can be identified by practising for the speaking interview, recording yourself, listening critically and evaluating yourself or getting your teacher to evaluate your performance. If you are making the same type of error, remedy the problem by doing some appropriate exercises.

Do not take the IELTS test if you are making lots of systematic errors. Systematic misuse of prepositions, subject/verb agreement, plurals, articles and word order will alert the examiner to your specific language problems.

Finally, remember that you do not have to speak perfect English to achieve a band score of 5 and above. However, you do need to impress the examiner. A positive, confident attitude will help.

GENERAL POINTERS:
- *Learn to speak clearly using appropriate vocabulary.*
- *Practise using different sentence structures.*
- *Practise paraphrasing – if you don't know a particular word, try to explain what you mean using different words.*
- *Get some strategies to repair the conversation if things go wrong.*
- *If you can't think of a real situation to talk about, imagine one; the examiner doesn't know or care if you are telling the truth, just that you are speaking.*
- *It is important to understand that your speaking cannot improve without much practice.*

GENERAL SPEAKING ADVICE

Do	Don't
Speak clearly and answer in full sentences.	Don't speak too softly.
Look at the examiner and maintain eye contact when possible.	Don't give yes or no answers.
Ask for something to be repeated if you do not understand what you are expected to do.	Don't try to be somebody else – just relax and answer the questions as well as you can.
Take the time to plan for Part 2.	Don't worry about speaking too much – the examiner will control the timing of your responses.
Vary the words and phrases you use.	Don't try to give a rehearsed speech.
Be well-mannered and respectful throughout the interview.	Don't stop trying throughout the interview.

IMMERSION IDEAS:

1. Become comfortable speaking in English – that means speaking in English as often as possible. Find friends or colleagues who will speak to you in English.

2. Practise the different parts of the interview with different people. Build your vocabulary and discuss different topics.

3. Familiarise yourself with different grammatical structures – practise using difficult structures like conditionals and standard introductory phrases like:

   "Well, in my opinion…".

4. Record yourself taking the practice test interviews and critically listen to yourself. If possible, ask a teacher or native-speaker to give you feedback on your performance. Focus on any systematic errors that appear.

5. Read about the speaking interview in *101 Helpful Hints for IELTS* and use the prepared questions to practise your interview style.

HOW TO TAKE THE PRACTICE TESTS

Before Taking the Practice Tests

- Read the Listening, Reading, Writing and Speaking Test Descriptions provided in this book.
- Read and practise the General Pointers included in the Test Descriptions.
- Familiarise yourself with the question types, specialised vocabulary and test format – all provided in this book.
- Find a quiet room.
- Allow three hours to complete each test.
- Ensure that you are not going to be interrupted.
- Take a highlighter pen, a pen or pencil and blank copies of a Listening Test Answer Sheet and a Reading Test Answer Sheet.
- Take paper to complete the writing tasks – IELTS will provide special pages for this, on the day of the actual test.
- Take a CD, cassette or audio player for the Listening Test and a recording device to use for the Speaking Interview.
- Take a clock or a watch.

During a Practice Test

- Strictly follow the timings for all parts of the IELTS test – that means doing the practice test under exam conditions.
- Complete the tests in the same order as they appear – Listening, Reading, Writing and then the Speaking Interview.
- Allow yourself 10 minutes to transfer your Listening Test answers onto the Answer Sheet.

After Taking Practice Test 1

- Check your answers to the Listening and Reading Tests with those provided in the Answer Keys section of this book.
- Refer to the *Study Guide to the 404 Essential Tests for IELTS* for Model Answers and extensive discussion of all the writing tasks.
- Listen carefully to the audio recording of your answers to the Speaking Interview questions and compare with the answers given in the *Study Guide to the 404 Essential Tests for IELTS*.
- Use the Score Analyser as a guide to determine your possible IELTS band score for each of the tests.

After Taking Practice Tests 1, 2 and 3

- Carry out the steps as outlined for Practice Test 1.
- Use the Score Analyser as a guide to determine if your errors are systematic.
- Focus on the errors that you are making – use the *Study Guide to the 404 Essential Tests* in conjunction with these tests; re-read appropriate sections from *101 Helpful Hints for IELTS* or *202 Useful Exercises for IELTS*.

After Taking Practice Test 4

- Carry out all of the above steps.
- Use the Score Analyser once again to determine your possible IELTS band score for each of the tests.
- Enrol for your IELTS test.

A motivated student, immersed in English and taking full-time intensive English classes, with support from an experienced teacher, should be able to improve by one full band scale in a ten to twelve week period.

PRACTICE TEST 1 - LISTENING

SECTION 1:   QUESTIONS 1 – 10

Listen to two students, Louise and Kerry, talking about their vacation.

Questions 1 – 4

Answer the questions below.
*Use **NO MORE THAN THREE WORDS OR A NUMBER** for each answer.*

Example:	Where did Louise spend her summer holidays?	.................................**Europe**......................

1   How much was a Eurailpass Youth Ticket?   ....

2   How many European countries did Louise's ticket allow her to travel to?   ....

   ....

3   Did the Eurailpass Youth Ticket include the train from London to Paris?   ....

   ....

4   How old must you be if you want to purchase a Eurailpass Youth ticket?   ....

   ....

Questions 5 – 10

Complete the notes below.
*Use **NO MORE THAN THREE WORDS** for each answer.*

Points that Louise makes about Eurail:

- easy to travel to small towns
- easy to meet (5) ....
- (6) .... with times of the trains
- night-trains had many (7) .... as passengers

Advice that Louise gives about Eurail:

- Don't take (8) .... bags
- Be (9) .... with your belongings
- Spend enough time in each country to experience (10) ....

SECTION 2: QUESTIONS 11 – 20

Questions 11 – 16

Complete the table below.
*Use **NO MORE THAN THREE WORDS** for each answer.*

Central City University - Student Support Services		
Academic Support Services	Course Content & Assessment Advisors (11)	- counselling re: course selection - language support
Library Services	Research & Resource Department Study Skills Department (13)	- assistance and advice for research and library use - assistance with arranging (12) .... - arrange computer logon and password
Administration Student Services	Administration Officers (14) .... Homestay Officer Student Employment Officer (15) .... Bookshop	- issuing student cards - independent accommodation advice - family-style accommodation advice - part-time and vacation employment - inquiries re: passports and visas - retail outlet
Student Union Services	Student Counselling Service Equal Opportunity Services Activity & Clubs Services	- counselling re: (16) .... problems - petitioning and sexual harassment - availability of clubs and activity schedules

Questions 17 – 20

Match the names of the buildings with the letters on the map below.

17   The Library   19   Bookshop   ....

18   Administration Building   20   International Student Advisor   ....

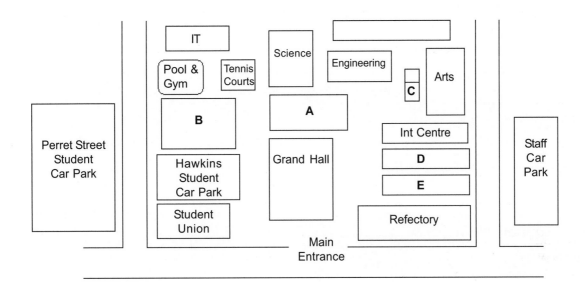

SECTION 3:   QUESTIONS 21 – 30

Questions 21 – 22

*Choose the correct letter from **A – C**.*

21   Rose's plan for the tutorial is to research and present

    A   the differences between male and female children.
    B   the different ways that male and female children are raised.
    C   the differences between male and female parenting.

22   The British experiments that Rose refers to in the conversation

    A   were carried out in 100 families.
    B   observed girls and boys who were raised identically.
    C   noted the different treatments males and females received.

Questions 23 – 26

*Choose **TWO** letters from **A – E**.*

23 & 24   This tutorial will

    A   require Marie and Rose to carry out research.
    B   interest the tutor and their classmates.
    C   be tested.
    D   help Marie to catch up on her research work.
    E   benefit other assessment that Rose and Marie have to do.

*Choose **TWO** letters from **A – E**.*

25 & 26   Before starting their preparation, Marie and Rose must

        A   catch up on other work.
        B   agree on the topic.
        C   get approval from the tutor.
        D   make an appointment to see a librarian.
        E   plan carefully for the next two weeks.

Questions 27 – 30

Complete the form below.
*Use **NO MORE THAN THREE WORDS** for each answer.*

Proposed Tutorial Topics	
Tutor: *Jim Clark* Department: **(27)**	Subject Code: *EC 101*
Topic: *'How The Sexes Differ'* Aims of tutorial: 1. *To show* **(28)** .... 2. *To show the differences are* **(29)**	
Day & Date of tutorial: *Tuesday 26th*	Time: *11 a.m.* Room: *B 1203*

A/V Equipment request

   ☐ TV   ☐ Tape Recorder
   ☐ Video   ☑ Overhead Projector

(30) How do you want to be notified of lecturer's approval?

   ☐ PHONE   ☐ LETTER
   ☐ FAX   ☐ IN PERSON

SECTION 4:   QUESTIONS 31 – 40

Questions 31 – 32

Complete the following sentences.
*Use **NO MORE THAN THREE WORDS** for each answer.*

31   The speaker identifies the following two differences between being a high school student and a university student:

     • the academic expectations of tutors and lecturers are ....

     • students must take responsibility for their own learning.

32 The speaker aims to get students to recognise exam stress and the way it can affect

....

Questions 33 – 36

Complete the table below.
*Use **NO MORE THAN THREE WORDS** for each answer.*

EXAM STRESS	
Signs	**Effective Management includes:**
Physiological: Increased pulse-rate Perspiration Breathing problems Problems with **(33)**	**(34)** .... breathing exercises
Psychological: Irrational **(35)** .... Panic	Be confident and **(36)** .... Be calm and analyse the questions.

Questions 37 – 40

Complete the following notes.
*Use **NO MORE THAN THREE WORDS** for each answer.*

37 Time needed to study effectively will .... according to individuals.

38 Time Management involves taking notice of the allocation of .... to exam questions.

39 To achieve good grades in examinations at university, you need to:

- have academic ability.

- be ....

- think clearly.

- observe time management practices.

40 Students wishing to develop their .... can attend next week's workshop.

PRACTICE TEST 1 - <mark>READING</mark>

PART 1

*First look at the Home Shopper advertisements (**Questions 1 – 6**):*

HOME SHOPPER ADVERTISEMENTS

1 EASEL

Would suit desk or tabletop. Suitable for aspiring artist or student. Adjustable angle and height. Excellent condition. $22. Telephone Jack on 0408 767 345

2 CASSETTE PLAYER

Sanyo with headset. In carton. Vintage 1972, but as new. Asking $25.

Phone 0406 543 287

3 MIRROR

Beautifully restored large oval mirror with oak carving panels and velvet inset. Circa 1800. Only $550.

Phone: 3665 4772

4 CHEST OF DRAWERS

4 drawers. 800mm H x 900mm L x 450mm W. Solid pine. Good condition. $65. Ring 7655 4300 between 9am and 5pm.

5 COLONIAL AMERICAN OAK TABLE

Solid extension table with strong, shaped legs. Built in late 1890s. Height 76 cm. Width 1.32 m. Very good condition. $2350 or nearest offer. Be quick – will sell. Phone Charlotte on 3389 6541

6 SEWING TABLE

This table has timber-moulded sides with steel legs. Storage space beneath. 2 fluorescent tubes to light the top. 1.9m x 1.6m. Ideal for any kind of craftwork. $150. Phone 0147 672 987 - evenings only.

Questions 1 –6

Choose the correct heading for each advertisement from the list of headings below.
*Note: **you may use any heading more than once**. Write the correct letter from **A – D** in boxes 1 – 6 on your Answer Sheet.*

List of headings
A Antiques
B Home Furnishings – General
C Home Entertainment
D Art and Craft

1 ....
2 ....
3 ....
4 ....
5 ,,,,,,,,,,,,,,,,,,,,
6 ....

*Now read the information below and answer **Questions 7 – 12**.*

P.L.S.
...the future is yours

For details access our website:
http://parkers.com.uk
OR email:
agentquery@parkers.edu.com.uk

Parkers Language School ... we have campuses around the world!

Flexible Worldwide Programme ➤ *Study anywhere in the world.*

Weekly Start Dates ➤ *Start your programme any Monday.*

All Language Levels ➤ *From beginner to advanced.*

Large Choice of Business and Academic Classes ➤ *Choose afternoon classes to suit your individual tastes.*

Try Before You Buy ➤ *Join a class to see if you like it.*

Cosmopolitan Atmosphere ➤ *Study with others from over 20 different countries.*

Social Calendar of Events ➤ *Tours and excursions to suit all tastes.*

Highly-satisfied Graduates ➤ *Visit our website and find comments from past students.*

Campuses:
Australia, UK, Canada, USA, Hong Kong, Taiwan, Europe

Questions 7 – 12

*Answer the questions below using **NO MORE THAN THREE WORDS OR A NUMBER** for each answer. Write your answers in boxes 7 – 12 on your Answer Sheet.*

7   When can students begin their course? ....

8   What kinds of afternoon classes can students select? ....

9   What can students do before they pay for a course? ....

10   How many nationalities are there in the school? ....

11   What kinds of social activities can the students take part in? ....

12   Where can potential students find more information? ....

Questions 13 –18 are based on the following information:

Website A Have you ever had a disaster in the kitchen? Have you ever made something that lacks a certain something? Do your cakes sink in the middle? Is your pastry soft and sticky instead of crispy and light? Contact Oliver's online advice website for all the answers. He will answer all your cooking queries quickly and clearly.	**Website B** Finding it hard to stay away from junk food? Is it difficult to eat the right kinds of food? Are you a sugar junky? You may need to subscribe and chat to people with similar needs and concerns. Motivate each other to stay away from bad foods and get out there and exercise.
Website C Visit the Annual Sydney Food Festival held on Friday 16th June. There is something for everyone with cooking demonstrations, handy cooking ideas, super sales on kitchen appliances and much more. Come and get your free sample bag and join in the fun. Tickets cost $30.00 per person. Book your tickets now online.	**Website D** Win two free tickets for you and a friend to go along and see Malcolm Watson and his cookery demonstration at the RNA Hall. Register your name for the competition and at the same time talk to Malcolm online before the show.
Website E Watch this instructional film online and learn the finer points of making pastry. Instructors from the famous Palais du Chef School of Cooking take you from beginner level to choux, filo, short and puff pastry at an advanced level.	**Website F** Join award winning chef John Syms in an online chat to celebrate the launch of his new book, Fresh is Best. With subjects ranging from easy pasta making to a seafood barbecue on the beach, go online to let John prove to you that creating sensational food need not be hard!
Website G Author Max Cannongate will be online to guide you in a series of lectures that help you to help yourself. He spends his time teaching and speaking about the ever-changing world of physical well-being and the challenge of fuelling your body with food that increases positive energy levels.	**Website H** In this fascinating online documentary film, producers Maurice Jurascovic and Janelle Stephenson have chartered the everchanging face of food throughout the last decade. With a special guest appearance from celebrity chef John Syms, this documentary is well worth a look.

Look at the website descriptions above *(A – H)* and the website addresses *(**Questions 13 – 18**)* below.

Match each website address with its most suitable description. Choose the correct letter from *A – H* and write it in boxes 13 – 18 on your Answer Sheet.

ANSWER

Example:	http://www.moviepastry.com	.......E.......
13	http://www.healthsupportgroup.com	....
14	http://www.cookingdemo.com	....
15	http://www.johnsymsfoodtalk.com	....
16	http://www.helpwithfood.com	....
17	http://www.selfhelp.com	....
18	http://www.ASFF.com	....

PART 2

Questions 19 – 30

*Read the information below about standards for working with children and answer **Questions 19 – 24**.*

Working With Children Fact Sheet

The Working With Children (WWC) Check creates a mandatory minimum checking standard across Australia. Its focus is on children and keeping them safe. It aims to prevent those who pose a risk to the safety of children from working with them, in either paid or volunteer work.

You will need to apply for a WWC Check if your work is in connection with one of the services, bodies, places or activities listed in Schedule A of this document, and your work usually involves, or is likely to usually involve, regular and direct contact with a child. People who undertake child-related work on no more than 5 days in a calendar year may choose whether or not to apply for a WWC Check. This is often called the "5 day threshold" and provides an exemption for unexpected work. Other exemptions also apply – it is your responsibility to find out if your job is listed on the exemption register at:

http://www.wwc.gov.au/register

You need only apply for a WWC Check once you are offered the child-related work. Unless you are in a licensed child care service where you will have to apply immediately upon starting, other jobs allow you to apply within 5 working days of starting.

If it is determined that a WWC check is required, an Application Guide and Form can be sourced via the WWC Check website. It must be completed and posted to the Child Welfare Department together with a copy of your driver's licence and the application fee. For those without a driver's licence, alternative forms of personal identification are just as acceptable and listed in Schedule B of this document.

If you pass the WWC Check, you will be sent your WWC Check Card in the mail. Employers must make sure employees have passed the WWC Check and may ask to see their cards as proof, however the Department of Justice will communicate the result of applications to employers. If your submission is refused, you are prohibited from working with children and could face up to 5 years in prison and a $60,000 fine if you continue to work in a child-related field of work.

The card remains current for 3 years, after which you will have to re-apply if you wish to continue in child-related work. The renewal process is the same as the initial application process, except you will receive a reminder letter one month before the expiry date. It is important that the WWC Screening Unit has your current address.

Questions 19 – 24

Do the following statements agree with the information given in the reading passage?
In boxes 19 – 24 on your Answer Sheet write:

YES	*if the statement agrees with the information*
NO	*if the statement contradicts the information*
NOT GIVEN	*if there is no information on this.*

Answer

Example:	Everyone who works with children has to apply for a WWC check.	...**NO**...

19   If your job is listed on the register, you do not have to apply for a WWC Check.   ....

20   You must apply for a WWC Check as soon as you know you have gained work at a child care centre.   ....

21   Applications can only be accessed online.   ....

22   A driver's licence is the preferred form of personal identification.   ....

23   It is the applicants' responsibility to inform their employers about the outcome of the application.   ....

24   Applicants who fail the check can appeal against the decision.   ....

*Read the information below and answer **Questions 25 – 30**.*

FLEXIBLE WORKPLACE POLICY

A flexibility policy is a document describing the rights and responsibilities of employees and employers in relation to flexible work arrangements, and it describes the steps for putting flexibility into practice. The process of creating a flexible workplace policy usually involves five key steps:

Begin by getting a general picture of the population within:

- **the Australian workforce** and the changes taking place within it;
- **the industry** and the trends of its workforce. In particular, research should be conducted into industry benchmarks in terms of flexibility arrangements; and
- **the workplace**; for example, finding out:

   o the proportion of women to men;
   o the average retirement age;
   o the average length of employment.

Next, try to gain a more detailed description or profile of your employees, such as how many have young children or plan to have children, or how many have elderly care or disability care responsibilities. This information can be obtained by conducting staff surveys, consultations, focus groups and interviews.

The next step involves getting the results of your research out there to the staff. There are many effective ways to ensure this happens, for example:

- **getting managers to talk to their staff** – choose people who understand what you're trying to do so they can support and implement the new programme;

- **sending out newsletters** to let employees know what's happening – a good idea for small to medium-sized businesses; and
- **using email and intranet** as a fast and efficient means of "talking" to employees in larger businesses.

The next thing you should do is make sure you have a good profile of your own workforce and a detailed understanding of employee needs. If you can do this, you'll have a better idea of which flexible work practices are best suited to your business. These may include flexible:

- **working hours** – for example, condensed hours or part-time work;
- **leave provisions** – for example, carer's leave, parental leave, annual leave;
- **work locations** – for example, working from home, teleworking; and/or
- **employment arrangements** – for example, job-sharing.

A very important and final step: you should have an in-built process to help you measure the success of your new policy and highlight improvements that may be needed. This may include outlining key performance indicators and work objectives, and setting a review period of three to six months, where feedback from employees, their managers and even clients is gathered to determine the impact of flexibility on the workplace.

Questions 25 – 30

Complete the summary below using the words listed in the box.

Write your answers in boxes 25 – 30 on your Answer Sheet.

strategies	Australian	aware	more
less	learning	feedback	statistics
interested	communicated	less rigid	evaluate
meetings	teams	record	lists

Creating a Workplace Flexibility Policy

A flexibility policy allows a business to create **(25)** .... work arrangements for its staff. Creating a flexibility policy is a step by step process. First, you will need to do some background research into the national workforce and your industry in general. Then, assess the needs of your own workers through surveys and **(26)** .... Once you have done this, you should make your staff **(27)** .... of the results of your research – this can be done verbally and via newsletters, for example. At the end of this process, you will have valuable **(28)** .... By this stage you will be ready to begin to develop **(29)** .... for introducing flexibility into your business. Finally, we recommend that you **(30)** .... the success of your policy in meeting the needs of your staff by reviewing it after six months.

PART 3

Read the passage below and answer **Questions 31 – 40.**

THE CROWN PALACE

The Crown Palace, or as we more commonly know it, the Taj Mahal, is probably one of the most recognisable buildings in the world. It has even been called the eighth wonder of the world. Everyone knows that it is in India, and most people probably know that it was built as a tomb for a dead empress, but do they know the exact history behind this amazing building?

In 1612, the Muslim Mughal emperor, Shah Jahan, married for the second time. His bride was Arjumand Banu Begam, although she is better known by her other name, Mumtaz Mahal. Despite the traditions of the time, this wedding was a real love match, the pair having fallen in love at first sight five years earlier, when they were fifteen. Mumtaz became inseparable from her husband, accompanying him on all his journeys and military campaigns. She had fourteen children by him, although bearing her fourteenth child, a girl, led to her tragic death at the age of 39.

Jahan was so overcome with grief that his hair and beard turned white in a matter of months after her death. Before her death, she had made Jahan make four promises to her: build a monument in her name; remarry; love and cherish their children; and finally, visit the tomb once a year on the anniversary of her death. Jahan only managed to fulfil two of these promises. However, luckily for the rest of the world, the monument was one of them.

How could he afford to build such a magnificent monument? Well, luckily for Jahan, the Mughals were extremely rich and very powerful. When he inherited the throne from his father in 1627, he also inherited great wealth. He used this wealth to ensure the Taj Mahal became the most incredible building of its time. He chose a site along side the River Jumna at Agra, once the capital of the Mughal Empire in the sixteenth century. The white marble used in its construction was transported by one thousand elephants, from 200 miles away, and inset with turquoise, jade, sapphires and amethyst. There are inscriptions from the Koran all round the Taj Mahal. Twenty thousand workers and artisans were involved in the project, which started the year after her death, and took twenty-two years to fully complete, during which time Jahan did indeed find himself a new bride.

Rumour has it that Jahan planned to build a mirror version of the Taj Mahal, on the other side of the River Jumna, but this would be built from black marble. Foundations and outline for a garden have been discovered in that vicinity, but the events which followed put a stop to any such building. Some years after the completion of the Taj Mahal, Jahan fell ill. His four sons by Mumtaz Mahal, who he had long since fallen out with, then turned on each other. The ensuing conflict left all but one of them, Aurangzeb, dead. He then overthrew his father in about 1658, and placed him under house arrest in Fort Agra for the rest of his life, barring him from visiting the palace. However, it is believed that, from his prison room, Jahan could look out on his incredible creation. On his death, some eight years later, his body was rescued by his daughter and taken across the river to be laid next to his beloved wife.

It is an interesting story, but what is it about this tomb that makes people from all corners of the world and all religions want to visit it - to risk the three-hour stomach-in-mouth road trip from Delhi to Agra? Simply, it is a breathtakingly beautiful sight. Walking through the main gate, you suddenly see a white marble arch which frames the Taj, acting like a veil covering a woman's face, slowly being lifted to reveal her true beauty. You can almost see visitors become awestruck as they view it for the first time. This is a strange occurrence in a time when we have seen most of the sights of the modern world in photographs and on television. It is rare for people to get a feeling of sheer amazement any more. However, this is exactly what you get when you see the Taj Mahal. Maybe it's just the summer heat, as some cynics would have you believe!

If you stay there for any length of time, you will see the different colours of the Taj Mahal. For at different times of the day, the tomb seems to change colour. From the pink of the morning, to the creamy white of evening, and the golden hue when the moon glows on it, the colours are a marvel to behold. Hindu traditions say that these colour changes depict the different moods of a woman. It is difficult to say if that is true, but one thing that is certain, if a building can have a gender, then the Taj Mahal is certainly feminine.

Questions 31 – 34

Complete the table below with words taken from the reading passage.

Use **NO MORE THAN THREE WORDS OR A NUMBER** *for each answer.*

Write your answers in boxes 31 – 34 on your Answer Sheet.

Event	Date
Agra was the capital of the Mughal Empire	*Example:* .... **16th Century** ....
Mumtaz Mahal and Jahan were born.	**(31)** ....
Jahan became emperor.	**(32)** ....
(33)	1658
Jahan died.	**(34)** ....

Questions 35 – 36

Answer the questions below using **NO MORE THAN THREE WORDS** *for each answer.*

Write your answers in boxes 35 – 36 on your Answer Sheet.

35 & 36   Which two of the promises to Mumtaz Mahal did Jahan not keep?

....

....

Questions 37 – 40

*Choose the correct letter from **A – D** and write it in boxes 37 – 40 on your Answer Sheet.*

37   What things adorn the Taj Mahal?

    A gemstones from 200 miles away
    B white marble elephants
    C religious pictures
    D precious stones

38   Jahan's prison room was

    A next to the Taj Mahal.
    B on the river bank.
    C on the other side of the river from the Taj Mahal.
    D in an imperial palace.

39   The journey from Delhi to Agra

    A is usually made by rail.
    B is frightening.
    C has wonderful scenery.
    D takes half a day.

40   The writer is surprised by people's reactions to first seeing the Taj Mahal because

    A they find the temperatures hot there in summer.
    B they have seen images of it before.
    C they have to walk through a veil.
    D they think it looks like a woman.

PRACTICE TEST 1 - WRITING

WRITING TASK 1

You should spend about 20 minutes on this task.

> *You want to go camping for a week with a friend.*
>
> *Write a letter to the campsite manager. In your letter*
>
> - *give details of when you would like to go*
> - *find out about the cost*
> - *ask them to send you some information about the campsite.*

Write at least 150 words.

You do **NOT** need to write any addresses.

Begin your letter as follows:

Dear Sir or Madam,

WRITING TASK 2

You should spend about 40 minutes on this task.

Write about the following topic:

> *Action movies with spectacular car chases are very popular with young people. It is often said that these sorts of movies lead to an increase in car accidents among young drivers as they try to copy what they have seen in the films.*
>
> *Do you agree that such movies increase the amount of bad driving? What can be done to encourage young people to drive more safely?*

Give reasons for your answer and include any relevant examples from your own knowledge or experience.

Write at least 250 words.

PRACTICE TEST 1 - SPEAKING

▶ **PART 1:**   (4 – 5 minutes) Introduction and (getting to know you) interview

Examiner: *Good morning. My name's ....*
And your name is...? And you're from...?
Can I see your passport please? Thank you.

- *Did you go to school in [your present country]...?*
- *What were your favourite subjects at school?*
- *Did you learn a language at school?*
- *What subjects interest you now?*
- *What do you plan to do in the future?*
- *How do you spend your free time?*
- *Do you like to relax with others or by yourself?*

Thank you.

▶ **PART 2:**   (3 – 4 minutes) Individual long turn (monologue)

Examiner: *Now I'm going to give you a card with some information about **FESTIVALS**.*
*You will have one minute to read the card and then I'd like you to talk about **FESTIVALS***
for one or two minutes. You can make some notes to help you if you wish. All right?

> **Describe a festival or cultural event that you celebrate in your country.**
>
> > **You should say:**
> >
> > **what the event is**
> >
> > **how often the event takes place**
> >
> > **who participates in the event**
>
> **...and explain why this festival or event is important to you.**

Examiner: *Would you like to start now?*

You give your talk and after 1 or 2 minutes the examiner will ask you a question or two.

- *Does everyone enjoy this festival?*
- *Are there many other festivals in your country?*

Thank you.

▶ **PART 3:**   (4 – 5 minutes) Two-way discussion (more abstract conversation)

Examiner: *Now I'd like to ask you a few more questions.*

- *How have cultural celebrations and festivals changed in your country?*
- *There is often a generation gap between children and their parents or grand-parents. Can traditions help to bridge this gap or do they make the gap wider?*
- *Are there any traditions in your own culture that you don't agree with or that you particularly like?*
- *Is it necessary for immigrants to adopt customs and festivals that are celebrated in their new country?*
- *What role does religion play in your own country?*

Thank you very much.
That's the end of the speaking test. Goodbye.

PRACTICE TEST 2 - LISTENING

SECTION 1:   QUESTIONS 1 – 10

Listen to the conversation between an external student and a Receptionist at Grisham College Counselling Office.

Questions 1 – 3

Complete the Student Profile below.
Use **NO MORE THAN THREE WORDS OR A NUMBER** for each answer.

STUDENT PROFILE – GRISHAM COLLEGE

Example:

    A New student
    B Current student
    C Past student - graduate

    ANSWER: **B**

Student Number: **(1)** .... - EXT

Name: Jack LARASSY   **Course**: Master of Linguistics
                                              School of Languages & Literacy

Date of Birth: **(2)** .... / .... / 1979

Address: **(3)** .... Avenue
                  CHELMSFORD, CM3 94Y

Questions 4 – 5

Complete the sign on the door of Grisham College Counselling Office below.
Use **NO MORE THAN TWO WORDS OR A NUMBER** for each answer.

Welcome to Student Services – Counselling Office

Office Hours: 8 a.m. to **(4)** ....

After Hours Entry: Use the **(5)** ....

                     and a Counsellor will let you in.

Telephone – 7893 4611

Listen to the conversation between the same student and the Student Counsellor.

Questions 6 – 10

Complete the Counsellor's notes.
*Use **NO MORE THAN THREE WORDS** for each answer.*

Student Name:	**Jack LARASSY**
Current Job	**Possible Future Job**
- working as a **(6)** .... - studying part-time	- research at university
Likes	**Advantages**
- the satisfaction - the six week summer holiday	- **(8)** .... teaching - increase in pay - would still have **(9)** .... - professionally beneficial
Dislikes	**Disadvantages**
- badly behaved students - lazy students - insufficient **(7)**	- **(10)** working .... - extra travel time

SECTION 2:   QUESTIONS 11 – 20

Questions 11 – 13

*Choose the correct letter from **A – C** for each answer.*

11   The problem that Constable Gray describes is

    A   women being robbed.
    B   thieves stealing bags from international tourists.
    C   Darlinghurst residents being robbed.

12   It is difficult to chase the thieves because

    A   they catch their victims by surprise.
    B   they choose older victims.
    C   the victims find it difficult to run as fast as the thieves.

13   The police have caught

    A   only two of the thieves.
    B   none of the thieves yet.
    C   almost all of the thieves.

Questions 14 – 15

*Choose **TWO** letters from **A – E**.*

14 & 15   Police advise the group of students to

    A   chase the thieves if it is safe.
    B   be more careful where they place their bags.
    C   avoid being alone in the area.
    D   avoid carrying too much money with them.
    E   use credit cards as much as possible.

Questions 16 – 20

Complete the following notes using **NO MORE THAN THREE WORDS** for each answer.

> If robbed, you should contact
> your **(16)** .... or
> Darlinghurst Police Station with
> the following details:
>
> - your full name
> - your contact telephone number
> - time of the incident
> - location of the incident,
>   for example,
>
> nearest **(17)** ....
>
> or name of **(18)** ....
>
> - **(19)** .... of item
>   that was stolen.
>
> Prevent illegal use of credit
> cards by **(20)** ....
> as soon as possible after the
> theft.

SECTION 3:   QUESTIONS 21 – 30

Questions 21 – 25

Choose the correct letter from **A – C** for each answer.

21   What is the purpose of Jane and Rick's meeting with the tutor?

    A   To collate information from their assignments
    B   To follow the correct procedure for the report
    C   To check on details of the report

22   What work still needs to be completed before doing the presentation?

    A   Conducting the actual questionnaire survey
    B   Collating data from the questionnaire and writing the report itself
    C   Analyzing the information gathered in the questionnaire

23   Which chart **A**, **B** or **C** shows the correct distribution of the 400 surveys Jane and Rick handed out?

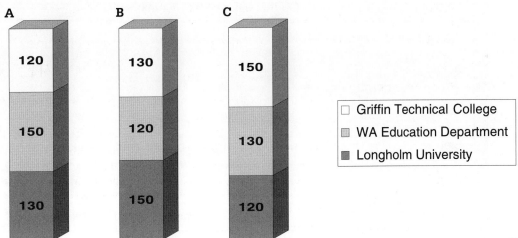

24 Why did Jane and Rick survey international students from three different institutions?

    A They didn't want to limit their responses to Longholm.
    B There weren't enough international students at Longholm.
    C They could access students of different ages at other institutions.

25 Which illustration (**A**, **B** or **C**) best shows the rates of responses in the pre-test and actual survey?

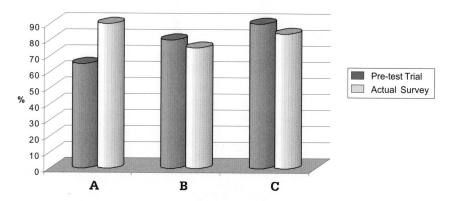

Questions 26 – 30

Complete the following flow chart. Insert the steps **A** *–* **F** *given in the box below.*

NOTE: there are more steps than you will need.

STEPS:
  A Distribute transmittal letter   **E** Present pre-test trial results
  B Rewrite unclear items   **F** Draw conclusions
  C Compile trial survey report   **G** Set objectives
  D Send reminders for overdue surveys

Steps for Survey and Presentation:

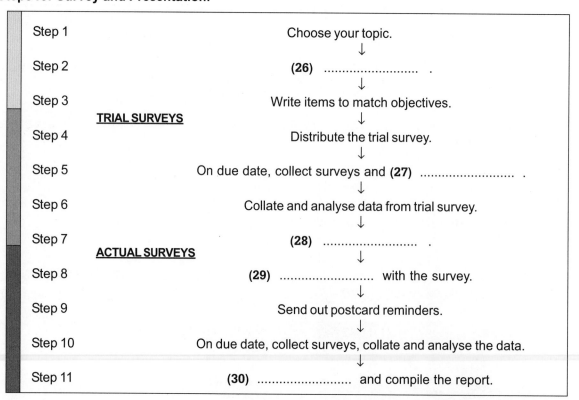

Step 1   Choose your topic.
↓
Step 2   **(26)** ....
↓
Step 3   Write items to match objectives.
           TRIAL SURVEYS   ↓
Step 4   Distribute the trial survey.
↓
Step 5   On due date, collect surveys and **(27)** ....
↓
Step 6   Collate and analyse data from trial survey.
↓
Step 7   **(28)** ....
           ACTUAL SURVEYS   ↓
Step 8   **(29)** .... with the survey.
↓
Step 9   Send out postcard reminders.
↓
Step 10   On due date, collect surveys, collate and analyse the data.
↓
Step 11   **(30)** .... and compile the report.

SECTION 4:   QUESTIONS 31 – 40

Questions 31 – 34

Complete the summary below.
*Use **NO MORE THAN THREE WORDS** for each answer.*

PROJECT MANAGEMENT

Last week's definition of project management:

Project Management has

- a clear **(31)** ....

- goals, budget and **(32)** ....

A project can be divided into **(33)** ....

The subject of today's lecture is **(34)** ....

Questions 35 – 39

Complete the table below.
*Use **NO MORE THAN THREE WORDS** for each answer.*

Elements of Stage 2	Considerations
Budget Planning	- most challenging element - try to plan **(35)** ....
Allocation of Time	- dependent on **(36)** .... - **(37)** .... used to identify tasks and schedules in units of work
(38)	- outlined in tender documents - help for this element can be obtained from **(39)** .... Manager

Question 40

Complete the sentence below.
*Use **NO MORE THAN THREE WORDS** for the answer.*

40   The three elements of Stage 2 will be examined in more depth in ....

PRACTICE TEST 2 - **READING**

PART 1

First read the passage below and answer **Questions 1 – 6**.

The Take-Me-Anywhere Camp Cooker

The Take-Me-Anywhere Camp Cooker is a cooker, which just as the name implies, can be used anywhere. You can use it with a range of fuels, and it offers the camper, or day-tripper, a choice of cooking methods.

It's made up of three sections. In the bottom section is the fuel source. You could build a wood fire, although for more convenience (if you find yourself on the beach with no available driftwood), it can be hooked up to a bottle for a gas flame. It is endorsed by the Royal Parks and Wildlife Service to be used in campsites if there is a fire ban, because the flame is totally enclosed in the bottom section. In addition it can be used with volcanic rocks.

The main section is large enough to fit a whole chicken, or large fish. This means you can put it on and leave it to cook while you relax or do a spot more fishing. There's a drip tray above the fire to catch the juices from whatever you're cooking. Above this, on either side, there are a couple of small baskets for you to wrap up your baked and roast vegetables. Just add a bit of butter in some foil and put them into the little roasting trays on the side. The lid, which is a big solid piece of stainless steel, is also multi-purpose, because it can double as another cooking surface for frying bacon, sausages and eggs.

This really is the complete camp cooker. At $770 it is certainly comparable with other good quality, less versatile camp cookers and it is definitely worth a look. Don't be deterred by its size, as it collapses down for storage, making it possible to fit into the boot of the smallest car.

Contact : Take-Me-Anywhere Camp Cooker   Ph : 1380 055 134

Questions 1 – 3

Label the diagram below.

Choose **NO MORE THAN THREE WORDS** from the passage for each answer. Write your answers in boxes 1 – 3 on your Answer Sheet.

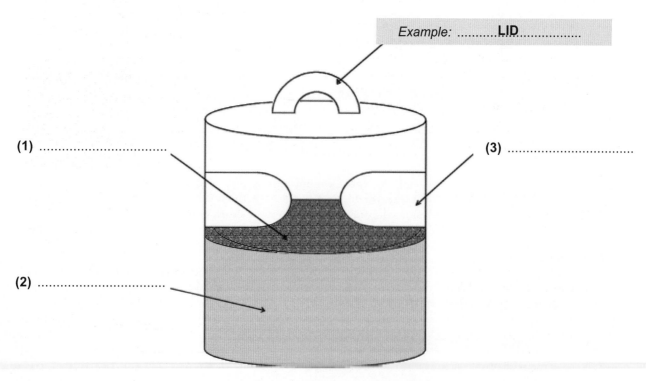

The Take-Me-Anywhere Camp Cooker

Questions 4 – 6

Choose the correct letter from **A – D** *to answer the questions below and write it in boxes 4 – 6 on your Answer Sheet.*

4 The Royal Parks and Wildlife Service

    A approves of this cooker.
    B needs to give permission to the camper to use the cooker.
    C will only allow it to be used when there is a complete fire ban.
    D sells the cooker.

5 The Go-Anywhere Camp Cooker

    A is cheaper than most camp cookers.
    B is more expensive than most camp cookers.
    C is about the same price as most other good camp cookers.
    D is the only specialist camp cooker available.

6 People who buy this

    A will need to have a big car.
    B will need to be campers.
    C will be able to cook lots of different meals.
    D All of the above.

Read the information below about the attractions that can be found at the Blue Mountains and answer **Questions 7 – 13**.

 # THE BLUE MOUNTAINS

Located less than two hour's drive from Sydney, the Blue Mountains offer a natural wonderland of untamed countryside, spectacular rock formations and native wildlife. There is plenty to see and do there. Here are just a few of the local attractions in the area.

Zigzag Railway
A historic tourist railway, utilizing steam trains and vintage diesel railmotors over a 7½ kilometre section of a former main railway line. The Zig Zag is a series of gently sloping ramps in the form of a letter 'Z' passing through 2 tunnels and over 3 magnificent sandstone viaducts.

Refreshments are available in the village of Clarence and there are picnic and barbecue rest areas. Open daily, except Christmas Day. Steam trains or rail-motors depart Clarence Station at 11.00 a.m., 1.00 p.m. and 3.00 p.m. The round trip takes 1 hour 20 minutes.

Jenolan Caves
Take a break from your world and visit the timeless seclusion of Jenolan Caves, where the beauty above and below ground is inspirational. Your enthusiastic and specially trained guide will describe the processes of nature that formed this natural wonder, as you explore chambers illuminated to highlight astonishing features. Over 3 kilometres of formed paths have been developed to provide a choice of cave tour options and themes to suit all ages and levels of fitness.

Additional tours operate during the school holidays, Saturday evenings and by appointment. Tours with durations from 1 to 2 hours, operate every day (including Christmas Day) from 10.00 a.m. Last tour departs at 5.00 p.m.

Scenic World

There are various things to do at Scenic World. Suitable for visitors of all ages is the Sceniscender, the steepest cable car in the Australia, which takes people on a three minute, 545 metre ride down into the rainforest. From high over the valley the Sceniscender descends smoothly into the ancient rainforest of the World Heritage listed Blue Mountains. The Scenic Railway is the world's steepest incline railway, descending 415 metres down the escarpment at a maximum grade of 52 degrees. This thrilling and unique ride passes through an 80 metre tunnel and a gorge.

The bottom platform of the Scenic Railway is connected by a 390 metre boardwalk to the Sceniscender bottom station. The boardwalk passes through a temperate rainforest and also passes the entrances to the old coal mines, where you can view an audio visual display. Beyond the Sceniscender bottom station you can walk a further 700 metres to the rainforest room, which is located deep in the valley. Altogether, Scenic World has approximately two kilometres of rainforest boardwalk.

The Scenic Skyway also at Scenic World, is the only passenger-carrying horizontal cable car in the Southern Hemisphere.

Scenic World also has a restaurant with a revolving floor, a new café and viewing area, a souvenir shop, a free car park and a 100-seat cinema. Open every day, including Christmas Day and Anzac Day.

(Source: Tourism New South Wales' website http://www.visitnsw.com.au.
Permission granted to use the above information on the Blue Mountains.)

Questions 7 – 13

*Look at the following statements (**Questions 7 – 13**) and the list of attractions (**A –D**) below.*

*Match each statement with the attraction it describes. Write the correct letter **A – D** in boxes 7 – 13 on your Answer Sheet.*

NOTE: you may use any letter more than once.

LIST OF ATTRACTIONS

A   Zigzag Railway

B   Jenolan Caves

C   Scenic World

D   All the above attractions

Answer

7   This attraction offers different choices of guided tours.   ....

8   You can buy a postcard here.   ....

9   You can make special arrangements to visit here
outside normal hours.

....

10   This attraction involves going underground.   ....

11   This attraction has special lighting.   ....

12   It is possible to buy a drink at this attraction.   ....

13   This attraction is closed on some days of the year.   ....

PART 2

Questions 14– 27

Read the passage below and answer Questions 14 – 20.

"Working From Home" Policy

An arrangement for an employee to work from home will only be entered into on a voluntary basis, which may be initiated by the employee. The company and the employee must mutually agree to the arrangement. An employee cannot be directed to work from home, and the company is under no obligation to approve a request from an employee to enter into a working from home arrangement.

Each application to work from home, whether as a permanent or temporary measure, will be considered on a case by case basis. Applications should be submitted a month in advance. Every application for a home-based work arrangement requires the approval of the Branch Head following the recommendation of the employee's supervisor. The Branch Head is responsible for ensuring that all of the requirements for approval have been satisfied prior to signing an application to work from home. In the event of a dispute about home-based work, the Director of Human Resources shall mediate, and, if necessary, arbitrate a decision.

Process for negotiating a home-based working arrangement

1. The employee will write an "Expression of Interest" and submit this to their Branch Head through the manager/supervisor for approval. If not approved, the employee's supervisor will discuss the reasons for refusal.

2. The Occupational Safety at Home Report should then be completed by the worker and submitted to the Occupational Safety Manager in Human Resources.

3. An agreement is then prepared, which is signed by the employee, the supervisor, and Branch Head. A copy is to be forwarded to Human Resources and placed on the employee's personnel file. This will detail the terms and conditions for working from home.

4. The appropriate Occupational Safety training and information shall be provided to employees who will be working from home by either the Branch's Safety and Health Representative or the Occupational Safety and Health Manager.

5. The supervisor should regularly review arrangements to work from home, especially during annual work performance reviews. In addition to this, a review of the agreement must also occur when:

   - there is a change of role or work location;
   - the combination of hours or the length of the arrangement needs to be renegotiated; and/or
   - the agreement expires.

Questions 14 – 20

Do the following statements agree with the information given in the reading passage?
In boxes 14 – 20 on your Answer Sheet write:

TRUE	*if the statement agrees with the information*
FALSE	*if the statement contradicts the information*
NOT GIVEN	*if there is no information on this.*

Answer

14 Both the business and the worker need to agree to the work arrangements.   ....

15 The business has to make a decision on the request within 4 weeks.   ....

16 The workers will be told why their requests have been turned down.   ....

17 Human Resources completes the Occupational Safety report.   ....

18   Human Resources negotiates the terms of the agreement.   ....

19   The workers will be given special instruction before they can start working
           from home.   ....

20   If the workers change their work days, they need to apply for the arrangement
           again.   ....

*Read the article below and answer **Questions 21 – 27**.*

Bradley Green Retail

Recruitment

The retail industry is very dynamic and provides a broad range of opportunities for job seekers. At Bradley Green Retail, we look at every application we receive as a chance to build and strengthen our team. Our recruitment process matches the needs of our stores with an applicant's skill set to find the perfect role for you!

To apply for a position with us, rather than handing your résumé to a nearby store, simply find us online at *www.bradleygreenrecruit.com* and click on *Current Vacancies* on the left hand toolbar. Search for a suitable position by looking at *Store Locations*. Once you have found a position of interest, select *Begin* to commence the application process and we will begin the process of matching your skills with our needs. Just register your general profile, fill out an application form and upload your résumé – it's that easy! To register you will need to have a current email address. You will receive a unique ID and password for future access to your candidate profile. Once you have filled out the application form, review it carefully before submission. If you do not find a position of interest on your first search, follow the steps to set up a Job Alert so that we can advise you when a suitable opportunity arises. After you submit your application, an acknowledgement of receipt will be sent to you via email.

If your application is successful, we will contact you to discuss the next stage in the recruitment process. The process may take two to four weeks depending on the position that you applied for and the number of applications that we received. If your application is successful, we will contact you directly and invite you to attend the *Group Gathering* with our Human Resources Department. Upon arrival, applicants will be asked to take a short basic mathematics test. Then, the job requirements will be outlined in more detail. Following this, applicants will be asked to perform role plays relevant to the type of position that they are seeking; for example, answering a customer's inquiry. Within seven days of the Group Gathering, successful applicants will be asked to attend the next stage in the recruitment process – a short interview with key personnel. This provides applicants with an opportunity to not only *answer* questions but *ask* any questions that they may have about joining Bradley Green Retail. Contact details for personal references will also be requested at this interview.

All candidates will be notified by email about the outcome of the interview process. Please check your email account frequently. Every application is kept in our database, so we can consider your details for future positions within Bradley Green Retail. You can refresh your details or withdraw your application at any time.

Questions 21– 27

Complete the flowchart below.

Choose NO MORE THAN TWO WORDS from the reading passage for each answer.

Write the answers in boxes 21 – 27 on your Answer Sheet.

BGR RECRUITMENT PROCESS:

Applications are made **(21)** ....

➡ Candidates choose an appropriate role after reading the **(22)** .... section.

➡ Next, the process should lead to an application that contains a **(23)** .... ,
a completed form and a résumé.

➡ If there are no roles of interest, the candidate should establish a **(24)** .... for
potential positions.

➡ Suitable candidates will attend the **(25)** .... and complete an assessment task.

➡ This is followed by short role plays such as **(26)** ....

➡ A week later, an opportunity is given to question the panel and provide **(27)** ....

➡ Details of those candidates who are unsuccessful in this round are held in the database for
potential roles.

PART 3

Questions 28 – 40 below are based on the following reading passage.

Asthma on the Rise

According to statistics from The Asthma Foundation, over the last twenty years, there has been a worldwide increase in childhood asthma. It dramatically affects the lives of one in four children and one in seven adolescents. It is also a major cause of hospitalisation in children.

Current medical opinion attributes modern environmental conditions to this worldwide increase. Dr. John Avent from the Childhood Diseases Society found that the homes of children who developed asthma had much lower levels of bacterial endotoxin, a substance which is found in dust – in other words, those homes were too clean. Whilst Dr. Avent doesn't recommend poor cleaning practices, he does maintain that there is an argument for parents allowing their children to play in less sanitary conditions and be less vigilant in this way about their environment.

Martin McFarlane of the Asthma Sufferers' Association has been involved in subsequent studies which have shown that children who had frequent respiratory infections were less likely to develop asthma as they grew older because of their early exposure to bacterial endotoxins. He maintains that this early exposure helped children to become stronger so they could avoid becoming overly sensitive to conditions that potentially trigger asthma. Dr. Leonie Bryce draws on this research and gives attention to recent studies into asthma which have suggested that the use of antibiotics may be instrumental in causing childhood asthma because early childhood infections protect children against asthma through the development of antibodies. As she says, "For this reason I am against the over-frequent use of antibiotics in treating childhood illnesses of any kind, particularly respiratory infections".

On a more positive note, more than half of childhood asthma sufferers will not have asthma as adults. However, research has identified a sliding scale of the most important risk factors that can tell a doctor whether a child will have asthma into adulthood. Firstly, young girls are more than two times more prone to having asthma into their adult years. This is a very high risk factor. The next risk factor of less importance but still representing a danger is whether a child has allergies and allergic reactions to a variety of products. Next in importance is whether the child was older than five when asthma first occurred. The most overwhelming risk factor, however, that contributes to asthma in adulthood is if asthma is common in the family (if a child has a parent or sibling with asthma). In this case, there is an extremely high chance that the child will develop asthma into adulthood. Since asthma is a major cause of hospitalisation in children, parents should try to be aware of what triggers their child's asthma and ensure that he or she is not exposed. For example, if house dust mites are a cause, parents should cover bed mattresses and pillows in vinyl covers. Weekly hot washing of bed linen is recommended and, if possible, blankets and quilts should be exposed to direct sunlight for several hours every week. Also parents are advised to avoid pillows and quilts made of feathers and wool. Smaller items can be put into a plastic bag in the freezer for four hours every fortnight and surfaces in the home should be dusted two or three times a week.

The National Asthma Council makes a number of recommendations for controlling asthma. Apart from parents ensuring that their child avoids the things that cause their asthma, their two most important tips are regular exercise and a healthy balanced diet. According to Dr Mary Tong, paediatric allergist and immunologist at the Royal Australian Hospital in Melbourne, there is no basis for the widely held view that dairy foods increase mucus production in the airways, making asthma worse. Dietary restrictions are not necessary unless there is a proven food allergy. Dr. Tong reiterates that dairy foods are an important source of calcium for strong teeth and bones and are particularly important for growing children.

Another recommendation is that parents should make sure that their family doctor is someone who has maintained a real interest in asthma – they should visit that doctor for regular review in order to check on their child's correct use of asthma medication. They should aim to know their child's symptoms and how best to treat them. To this end, the National Asthma Council recommends that parents of young children with asthma develop an Asthma Action Plan. The Plan, created in conjunction with their family doctor, should outline ways to monitor the asthma – by keeping a diary of asthma symptoms, for example. It should also outline the ways in which a parent can recognise worsening asthma, what to do when this happens and how and when to get medical help quickly.

By following the recommendations, parents are given the tools with which to manage, and even control, their child's asthma.

Questions 28 – 31

*Look at the following questions (**Questions 28 – 31**) and the risk factors below.*

Answer each question by choosing the most suitable risk factor.

*Write the correct letter **A – D** in boxes 28 – 31 on your Answer Sheet.*

RISK FACTORS

A   the child is a girl

B   the child is in a family where asthma is common

C   the child has allergies

D   the child was more than 5 years old when he/she first got asthma

---

28   Which is the highest risk factor? ....

29   Which is the second highest risk factor? ....

30   Which is the third highest risk factor? ....

31   Which is the least important risk factor? ....

Questions 32 – 35

Complete the summary of the reading passage.

*Choose **NO MORE THAN THREE WORDS** from the passage for each answer.*

Write your answers in boxes 32 – 35 on your Answer Sheet.

Tips for Parents

Manage your child's asthma by:

Taking away the **(32)** .... in your child's environment that can make asthma worse.

Making sure your child gets regular exercise.

Ensuring your child eats a balanced diet.

Finding a doctor with a/an **(33)** ....

Making sure your child uses his/her **(34)** .... correctly.

Knowing your child's symptoms and how best to treat them.

Developing a/an **(35)** .... with your doctor.

Questions 36 – 40

*Look at the following statements (**Questions 36 – 40**) and the list of people below.*

*Match each statement with the person who made it. Write the correct letter **A – F** in boxes 36 – 40 on your Answer Sheet.*

NOTE: you may use any letter more than once.

36   Children can manage their asthma by being active and eating good food.   ....

37   Antibiotics are bad for babies and young children.   ....

38   Having lots of coughs and colds early in life can mean children are able to build up their immune system.   ....

39   Foods rarely make asthma worse.   ....

40   The incidence of asthma in the world today is increasing.   ....

LIST OF SPEAKERS

A   Dr. John Avent

B   Martin McFarlane

C   Dr. Leonie Bryce

D   Dr Mary Tong

E   The National Asthma Council

F   none of the above

PRACTICE TEST 2 - WRITING

WRITING TASK 1

You should spend about 20 minutes on this task.

> *On your return from Sydney, where you attended a conference, you accidentally left a bag in the taxi at the airport. Among other things, it contained a copy of the research paper you gave at the conference. You rang the Lost Property Department of the taxi company but they were rude and unhelpful.*
>
> *Write a letter to the Lost Property Department at the taxi company. In your letter*
>
> - *advise them of the circumstances in which you lost your bag*
> - *provide details about the bag and its contents*
> - *complain about their lack of help in this matter.*

Write at least 150 words.

You do **NOT** need to write any addresses.

Begin your letter as follows:

Dear Sir or Madam,

WRITING TASK 2

You should spend about 40 minutes on this task.

Write about the following topic:

> *People often believe that great musicians are born and not made.*
>
> *Do you agree that we are born with much of our ability, or are there other factors, such as family and environment, that determine success?*

Give reasons for your answer and include any relevant examples from your own knowledge or experience.

Write at least 250 words.

PRACTICE TEST 2 - SPEAKING

▶ **PART 1:**   (4 – 5 minutes) Introduction and (getting to know you) interview

Examiner: Good morning. My name's ....
And your name is...? And you're from... ?
Can I see your passport please? Thank you.

- *Who do you live with in [your present country]... ?*
- *Can you describe your room to me?*
- *What do you do to relax in the evenings?*
- *Why are you taking this speaking test?*
- *Do you enjoy studying English?*
- *Can you remember your first English lesson?*
- *What's you favourite time of the year?*

Thank you.

▶ **PART 2:**   (3 – 4 minutes) Individual long turn (monologue)

Examiner: Now I'm going to give you a card with some information about **FAMILY AND FRIENDS**.
You will have one minute to read the card and then I'd like you to talk about **FAMILY AND FRIENDS** for one or two minutes. You can make some notes to help you if you wish. All right?

Describe a special friend or family member.

You should say:

who the person is

why they are so special

what you usually do together

...and describe a special time you have spent with that person.

Examiner: Would you like to start now?

You give your talk and after 1 or 2 minutes the examiner will ask you a question or two.

- *Do you see your family often?*
- *Do you spend more time with your family or friends?*

Thank you.

▶ **PART 3:**   (4 – 5 minutes) Two-way discussion (more abstract conversation)

Examiner: Now I'd like to ask you a few more questions.

- *Do you think the family unit is less important in modern life now?*
- *Should children look after their parents when they get older?*
- *What qualities should a parent have?*
- *Do you think you are a good friend? Why?*

Thank you very much.
That's the end of the speaking test. Goodbye.

PRACTICE TEST 3 - LISTENING

SECTION 1:   QUESTIONS 1 – 10

Listen to the conversation between two friends who are talking outside an examination room.

Questions 1 – 2

Choose the correct letter from **A – C** for each answer.

> **Example:** Why is Peter tired?
> > **A**   The exam was long.
> > **B**   He got up early this morning.
> > **C**   He studied until late the previous night.
>
> ANSWER: **C**

1   Why can't Peter relax over the three-week vacation?

>   **A**   He needs to earn some money.
>   **B**   He's worried about next semester.
>   **C**   He can't afford to go away.

2   What does Crystal plan to do on the holidays?

>   **A**   She's going to visit her family.
>   **B**   She's going to get a job.
>   **C**   She hasn't got any idea.

Questions 3 – 5

Listen to the directions and identify the place names of Questions 3 – 5 on the campus map below. Choose your answers from the list of place names in the box.

NOTE: there are more place names listed than you will need.

List of Place Names:	I Block
	C Block
	Student Employment Office
	Student Canteen
	Bookshop

3   ....

4   ....

5   ....

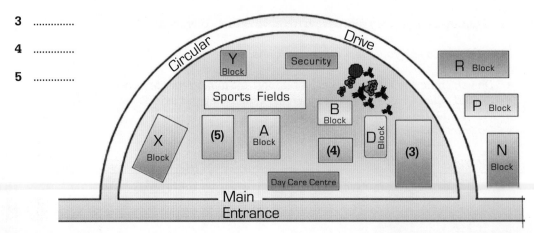

Questions 6 – 7

Complete the sentences below.
*Use **NO MORE THAN THREE WORDS OR A NUMBER** for each answer.*

6   First, Peter and Crystal must have a/an ....

7   Peter and Crystal arrange to meet at .... on Friday.

Questions 8 – 10

Complete the table below.
*Use **NO MORE THAN ONE WORD OR A NUMBER** for each answer.*

	Surname	Contact Phone Number	Student Number
Peter	(8)	(9)	B 723466
Crystal	Lu	~	(10) ....

SECTION 2:   QUESTIONS 11 – 20

Questions 11 – 13

*Choose the correct letter from **A – C** for each answer.*

11   The main aim of the festival spokesperson at the gathering is to
    A   welcome visitors to Brisbane.
    B   give away some tickets to the Brisbane Festival.
    C   provide information regarding the Festival.

12   The program for the Brisbane Festival includes performers from
    A   local and international destinations.
    B   Australian, Asian and European destinations.
    C   Australian and international destinations.

13   The Brisbane Festival will schedule activities and performances
    A   at indoor and outdoor venues.
    B   over 290 days.
    C   in traditional performance centres around the city.

Questions 14 – 20

Complete the table below.
*Use **NO MORE THAN THREE WORDS OR A NUMBER** for each answer.*

Type of Activity	Date	Time	Name of Event	Venue
Music	8 Sept	8 p.m.	Israel Philharmonic Orchestra	Performing Arts Centre
Drama	(14)	6:30 p.m.	Monkey	Power House
(15)	11 Sept	8 p.m.	Sumi Jo with Queensland Orchestra	Performing Arts Centre
Music	Wed - Sat	~	(16)	City Gardens
Visual Arts	From (17)	~	Asia-Pacific Triennial	Art Gallery
Drama	15 Sept	6 p.m.	Slava's Snowshow	(18) ....
Music	20 Sept	8 p.m.	Barbara Fordham in concert	(19) ....
Poetry	From 22 Sept	~	Poetry Festival	~
Writing	4 Oct - 6 Oct	~	Writers' Festival	~
Music	6 Oct	6 p.m.	(20) Opera	City Gardens

SECTION 3:   QUESTIONS 21 – 30

Question 21

*Choose the correct letter from **A – C**.*

21   Who are Nancy and Jenny?

    A   students from Singapore and Malaysia
    B   students who have travelled to Singapore and Malaysia
    C   students who have researched Singapore and Malaysia

Questions 22 – 24

Complete the table below.
*Use **NO MORE THAN THREE WORDS OR A NUMBER** for each answer.*

COUNTRY PROFILES		
	Singapore	**Malaysia**
Area of land:	630 square kilometres	**(22)** .... square kilometres
Population:	**(23)**	Under 24 million
Approximate ethnic mix:	**(24)** .... Chinese 14% Malay 9% Indian	65% Malay (Bumiputera) 26% Chinese 8% Indian

Questions 25 – 30

Complete the sentences below.
*Use **NO MORE THAN THREE WORDS** for each answer.*

25 Australia's relationship with Singapore has been ....

26 Trade between Singapore and Australia is ....

27 Singapore and Malaysia share .... and .... as their top trading partners.

28 There has been an increase in .... between Australia and Malaysia.

29 Nancy found that the government in Singapore invested a lot in ....

30 Nancy and Jenny thought that Malaysia has a good balance of .... customs.

SECTION 4: QUESTIONS 31 – 40

Questions 31 – 32

Complete the notes below.
*Use **NO MORE THAN THREE WORDS** for each answer.*

31 For .... there have been vegetarians.

32 True vegans will only eat food which ....

Questions 33 – 34

*Choose **TWO** letters from **A – E**.*

33 & 34 Which two reasons are NOT given in the lecture for adopting vegetarianism?

    A religious beliefs
    B environmental reasons
    C peer pressure
    D cost
    E social acceptance

Questions 35 – 36

Choose **TWO** letters from **A – E**.

35 & 36 Which two health issues are NOT used in the lecture to promote vegetarianism as healthy?

    A   reduced heart disease
    B   lower risk of contracting cancer
    C   reduced blood sugar levels
    D   fewer weight-related problems
    E   lower risk of stomach ulcers

Questions 37 – 39

Complete the following table.
Use **NO MORE THAN THREE WORDS** for each answer.

VITAMIN AND MINERAL INTAKE

	Available to non-vegetarians in...	Available to most vegetarians in...	Available to lacto-vegetarians and vegans in...
Iron	meat	spinach, prune juice or (37)	~
B12	meat, fish and dairy products	dairy or soy products and (38)	vegetable margarines, soy products and some (39) ....

Question 40

Complete the sentence below.
Write **NO MORE THAN THREE WORDS** for your answer.

40   The website address given for the UK Vegetarian Society is ....

PRACTICE TEST 3 - READING

PART 1

*Look at the information below about Fire and Rescue Services and answer **Questions 1 – 6.***

■ FIRE & RESCUE SERVICE ■

offers

A FIRE SAFETY INSPECTION OF YOUR HOME

<<<*FREE OF CHARGE*>>>

- Fire and Rescue Service is offering a **FREE** fire safety inspection for your home.
- The inspection is carried out by the operational crew from your local Fire Station.

Inspections provide practical advice on how to increase the fire safety within your home by identifying potential fire safety hazards. The visit will take approximately 45 minutes, at the end of which you will be supplied with a checklist to help you improve fire safety.

All home owners and renters of houses, flats, units, caravans and sheds are eligible and you can register by telephoning your local fire station and leaving your details.

After registration, we will ring you back and book a time and a date – we work 7 days a week. Our appointment is, of course, dependent on any emergency work that may arise in the course of the week.

This programme is aimed at reducing the occurrence of death and injury due to fires and accidents in the home. You are given practical advice on how to remedy potential problems should they occur. We also give advice on installation, positioning and maintenance of smoke alarms and extinguisher positioning and use. Home evacuation planning is also an area we can advise you on in order to prepare you for possible emergency fire situations. We talk about all of this, along with all other aspects of safety. At the end of the inspection, your home may be eligible to have a free smoke alarm fitted.

Two members from our operational crew at your local Fire Station will conduct the inspection. They will arrive in the local fire truck with other crew members who are happy to show the children over the Fire Engine while the inspection is being carried out.

PHONE NOW 1365 977

**REGISTER TODAY FOR YOUR
FREE INSPECTION**

Questions 1 – 6

*Using information from the reading passage, write if the statements (**Questions 1 – 6**) below are:*

> **TRUE**   *if the statement agrees with the information*
> **FALSE**   *if the statement contradicts the information*
> **NOT GIVEN**   *if there is no information on this.*

Write your answers in boxes 1 - 6 on your Answer Sheet.

		Answer
Example:	The fire and rescue service crew are volunteers.	**NOT GIVEN**

1	The fire and rescue crew advise people on how to have safer homes.	....
2	You can make an appointment for an inspection when you register.	....
3	The date of the appointment may have to be changed.	....
4	When the inspection is finished, you get a free smoke alarm.	....
5	Two members of the fire and rescue team come to your home.	....
6	Fire and rescue services are usually free.	....

Questions 7 – 13

*Look at the upcoming events at The University of Pullenvale and answer **Questions 7 – 13**.*

THE UNIVERSITY OF PULLENVALE

UPCOMING EVENTS INCLUDE

U.P. CHOIR TRIALS

If you are interested in recreational singing, fun times with a group of like-minded people and the chance of weekend travel, then come to the U.P. choir trials. If you qualify for entry into our well-respected university choir, you will be able to enjoy all this and more.

When: September 11.
Where: Room 8B, The Forum.

UNICLEAN AWARENESS DAY

The University of Pullenvale is gearing up for its first UniClean Awareness Day – to be held from 11 a.m. – 7.30 p.m. on September 5. Activities will include group rubbish collecting, information sessions, a free sausage sizzle, launch of the Ban the Litter project, displays of campus kindergarten artwork, reverse garbage sculptures, and a public lecture.

U.P. STOREWIDE SALE

The U.P. Bookstore is having a storewide sale where all merchandise – books, clothing, magazines, stationery, cards and giftware – are reduced by 50%. The sale will run for a limited time only (3/9 – 18/9) and the discount will only apply to items in stock.

FUNDRAISING EVENTS

PALLON HOUSE EVENTS

Dinner Concert and Circus Spectacular
Be amazed by the spectacular aerial antics of the Stantonville Circus Set with their daring acrobats and

tightrope walkers. Be thrilled by the fantastic costumes and wonderful music. A night to remember - $100 all inclusive.

When: Friday 12 September, 8 p.m.
Where: The Green Room, Pallon House.

Vivaldi Concert
Enjoy Vivaldi's stunning musical masterpiece, "The Four Seasons" performed by the Sydney Orchestral Group and accompanied by fireworks and dance. Free admission.

When: Friday 19 September, 7 p.m.
Where: Pallon House Gardens – "The Arena".

SCHOOL MUSIC CONCERT

As a major feature of the 2002 Festival of the Classics, the University of Pullenvale will present Schubert's Unfinished Symphony with conductor Flynn Richardson and Hayden's Harmoiniemesse under the baton of Robert Harris. Tickets at the door. Adults $20, Concession $15.

When: Sunday 14 September, 8 p.m.
Where: Concert Hall.

Questions 7 – 13

Answer the questions below using **NO MORE THAN THREE WORDS**. *Write the answers in boxes 7 – 13 on your Answer Sheet.*

7 Which event will interest me if I would rather participate in music than be a spectator?

....

8 Which event will be best for cheap musical entertainment?

....

9 Which event will interest me if I am aware of environmental issues?

....

10 What is the first scheduled event?

....

11 The Bookstore does not stock the book I need but they have ordered it for me. It costs $40.00. How much will I have to pay?

....

12 Besides the orchestra, what can we see when we go the Vivaldi concert?

....

13 Which musical event gives student discount?

....

PART 2

Read the memo below and answer *Questions 14 – 21*.

INTER-OFFICE MEMO

Date: 1 July   To: All Employees

                                From: Ms Mary Anne Muck, H.R. Department

Re: Buy Recycled Policy

As you are aware, our company is dedicated to the concept of recycling. However, recycling is more than just placing certain materials in a special bin. The recycling loop is complete only when materials that you have separated for recycling are processed and remanufactured into new products, which are then sold. This means that recycling works only when consumers, businesses and organisations purchase products made with recycled material.

With this in mind, we are implementing an innovative policy in all of our offices to buy supplies that are made from recycled content. We are doing things such as buying recycled printer paper, envelopes, paper towels, paper cups, napkins and cardboard.

After a thorough check of the performance of recycled content products, the company is keen to begin the new policy. We are sure that the constant upgrading of manufacturing technology has enabled most recycled products to compete – both in terms of price and quality – with products made from original materials.

The company wishes to show that it is working towards a sustainable environment, and encourages employees, before ordering office goods, to always look at the level of post-consumer recycled content in a product: this is the material that has been collected from consumers and reprocessed. Manufacturers often have pre-consumer material in their total recycled content calculation: this material may be manufacturing scraps that were never used in the consumer market. Thousands of recycled products are available today. Many items from paper to printer cartridges to motor oil are available with recycled content. In fact, many contemporary stationery catalogues already include a variety of recycled products, so you may be able to find what you need and 'buy recycled'.

With everyone's participation, I am confident that we can make a strong commitment to buy products that contain recycled content. And by getting staff to do this in the workplace, we may encourage you to think more deeply about doing this at home.

If you have any questions, please call one of the HR Team on extension 45.

Questions 14 – 21

Complete the sentences below. Choose **NO MORE THAN THREE WORDS** from the reading passage for each answer. Write your answers in boxes 14 – 21 on your Answer Sheet.

14   Ms Muck believes that successful recycling is when goods are ....

15   The new strategy being outlined is based on the type of .... to be bought.

16 The company has confirmed the .... of the goods.

17 As a result of improved machinery for recycling, competition based on ....
is now possible.

18 The aim of the company is to assist in maintaining the ....

19 Staff are urged to check if pre-consumer items such as .... are included in
the complete recycled content.

20 Staff are advised that up-to-date .... could be consulted before buying
goods.

21 Ms Muck is hopeful that employees will become motivated to purchase items with
.... when they are not at work.

Questions 22 – 27

*Read the passage below and answer **Questions 22 – 27**.*

The Work Experience Placement Programme

*** Long-term unemployment impacts on communities both socially and economically. The long-term unemployed often have difficulty in gaining employment due to a number of factors such as a loss of confidence and motivation, a lack of recent work experience, or simply, inappropriate skills.

A The Work Experience Placement (WEP) programme is a new government initiative. Through the process of the government placing eligible workers into organisations for the purpose of work experience, it is hoped that those people will gain a greater insight into the working environment as well as acquire additional skills that will ultimately lead to sustainable ongoing employment.

B Most organisations are eligible to be a part of WEP with the exception of those offering only volunteer positions and those that promote or condone any form of unlawful discrimination. It goes without saying that organisations involved in any form of illegal activity are not considered suitable. The most appropriate organisations will be those that offer a reasonable prospect of employment at the end of the WEP placement; also those organisations willing to train the person doing work experience and provide a safe work environment.

C The placement depends greatly on the host organisation and the type of work involved. For example, larger organisations may have the capacity to place the worker into several different work environments within the company – on the factory floor, in the office, as part of a sales team. In this kind of environment, the potential for a longer period of placement is higher than, say, in a small local organisation with fewer employees. Therefore, work experience placements can vary.

D WEP allows host organisations to assess how well a worker picks up skills and operates in the work environment, at no cost to the host. This means host organisations can try somebody out before hiring them, and workers gain experience and show how they can be a valuable potential employee for hosts.

E Workers will continue to receive income support payments from the government and not wages from the WEP organisation. This is because neither party is entering into an employer/ employee agreement. Nor will participants be eligible to be paid for superannuation or receive leave entitlements from the organisation. If the host decides to employ the worker, the work experience placement automatically ends, and a normal employer/employee agreement begins.

F The Work Experience Placement programme will be open to disadvantaged job seekers, including those who have been unemployed for more than 12 months, and those who have had previous employment in positions which are no longer economically sustainable. Some parenting payment recipients may also be able to participate. Please refer to your nearest Providers of Australian Government Employment Services (PAGES) for further information regarding eligibility.

*The reading passage has six paragraphs (**A – F**) .*

Choose the correct heading for each paragraph from the list of headings below.

*Write the correct number **I – IX** in boxes 22 – 27 on your Answer Sheet.*

Questions 22 – 27

LIST OF HEADINGS

I	Basis of the Work Experience Placement Relationship
II	Benefits for Work Experience Placement Participants
III	Work Experience Placement Aims
IV	Variety in Placements
V	Duration of Work Experience Placement
VI	Workplace Reforms
VII	Employee Payment Options
VIII	Suitable Host Organisations
IX	Eligible Workers

Answer

22	Paragraph A	....
23	Paragraph B	....
24	Paragraph C	....
25	Paragraph D	....
26	Paragraph E	....
27	Paragraph F	....

PART 3

Questions 28 – 40 are based on the reading passage below.

Genetically Modified Foods –
Frankenstein foods or the future of agriculture?

Since man began farming, food has been modified by selective breeding and cultivation. However, in 1972 Paul Berg, a biochemist at Stanford University, discovered how to join the DNA of two organisms to make the first combined DNA molecule. This was the beginning of transgenic technology. This new technology was greeted with great praise and interest, but was closely followed by ethical and safety concerns. What effect would altering the DNA of food have on humans who consumed it? Over thirty years later, the technology has developed greatly, but the concerns surrounding it have not disappeared.

There is no doubt that the majority of people are wary of genetically modified (GM) foods. Whether or not this is as a result of watching too many horror movies, which have mutated animals and plants wreaking havoc on mankind, is difficult to know but everyone, including GM supporters, remain a little cautious. Nonetheless, most people have strong views either one way or the other, but more and more the lines are being divided geographically, with the United States (along with Argentina, China and Canada) firmly in one corner and Europe in the other.

The United States and Europe have long been in dispute over the development and use of GM foods. The US President even got involved in the ongoing debate blaming Europe's "unfounded, unscientific fears" about the use of GM foods, for the hesitancy of famine ravaged Third World countries in adopting the new technology. (In 2002, Zambia, despite millions of its people facing food shortages, turned away thousands of tonnes of maize from aid agencies because it had been genetically modified.) This attack was not well received by European countries still smarting from the effects of Mad Cow Disease – effects that were not realized until more than thirty years after it had been declared that dead sheep had been used as cow fodder. It is no wonder that Europe is not rushing to get involved in GM food.

However, it is worth remembering that Americans have been growing and eating GM foods for more than ten years. Up to now there has been no undue increase in the cases of strange diseases in humans, nor have we seen a growth in superweeds caused by the spread of GM pollen. To them, Europe is being backward and is failing to move with the times.

For the past four years Europe has had a ban on GM food. However, that could all change if the European Parliament goes ahead and approves strict laws regarding the labeling and traceability of foods which contain GM ingredients. Big biotech companies are holding their breath for the results, which could mean billions of dollars to them in increased profits. On the other hand, international trade could be seriously affected if Europe doesn't change its stance on GM food. Countries that could benefit from producing GM crops and food may hesitate to use the new technology if their GM harvests are likely to be banned from the huge European market.

So if Europe does remove its ban on GM food, what kinds of things could we find available? One famous GM food, Golden Rice, is seen as a breakthrough in preventing blindness caused by a diet deficient in Vitamin A. Golden Rice is a combination of rice and a gene from a daffodil (a yellow-flowering bulbous plant). The daffodil gene is rich in beta-carotene, which when absorbed by the body produces Vitamin A. Another GM product includes a type of corn and cotton that poisons and kills pests that usually feed on the crop. Proponents of GM food claim that this could lead to the effective removal of pesticides and insecticides from farming. This, in turn, could result in less pollution of the soil and cheaper costs for farmers. Scientists in Japan have started producing rice that has been genetically modified to stop allergies like hay fever. In addition, they say that this GM rice can help to reduce cholesterol levels. Other scientists are also working on growing bananas and rice that have been given extra proteins in the hope that this will help to reduce cases of malnutrition. My personal favourite is the development of an onion that will not make you cry when you chop it!

GM food is a huge, and potentially lucrative, industry that businesses are investing millions of dollars into. It is also an industry that will undoubtedly influence our lives in the future. Only time will tell whether this technology can be used without causing additional problems for humans and the environment.

Questions 28 – 33

Using information from the reading passage, write if the statements (**Questions 28 –33**) below are:

> **TRUE**   if the statement agrees with the information
> **FALSE**   if the statement contradicts the information
> **NOT GIVEN** if there is no information on this.

Write your answers in boxes 28 –33 on your Answer Sheet.

		Answer
28	Modification of food commenced after Paul Berg's discovery in 1972.	....
29	As GM foods have developed, people's fears about GM foods have lessened.	....
30	Canada and Argentina grow GM crops.	....
31	Europe is concerned about the long term effects of GM foods.	....
32	Many people died in Zambia because it refused aid containing GM maize.	....
33	America has had no serious problem so far from GM foods.	....

Questions 34 – 40

Complete the summary below using **NO MORE THAN THREE WORDS.** Write your answers in boxes 34 – 40 on your Answer Sheet.

Although GM foods are currently (34) .... in Europe, you could soon be able to buy food which has been genetically modified as long as any (35) .... are clearly marked on the label. This could lead to an upturn in profits for (36) .... and an increase in (37) .... for some developing countries.

Some GM products currently under development include Golden Rice, which can help combat (38) .... Others could mean that farmers would no longer require (39) .... to grow crops. (40) .... have been added to some crops to prevent disease caused by lack of food.

PRACTICE TEST 3 - WRITING

WRITING TASK 1

You should spend about 20 minutes on this task.

> *You applied for and paid to attend a series of three work-related seminars due to begin next week. Unfortunately you have just received news that your father has been taken ill suddenly and you will have to return home to Hong Kong to see him. You are disappointed as the seminars would have been very helpful to your career and you were looking forward to attending.*
>
> *Write a letter to the owner of the hotel. In your letter*
>
> - *advise them of your inability to attend, express your disappointment and apologise*
> - *ask whether you can attend the seminars at a later date*
> - *if there are no more seminars this year, ask for a refund.*

Write at least 150 words.

You do **NOT** need to write any addresses.

Begin your letter as follows:

Dear Sir or Madam,

WRITING TASK 2

You should spend about 40 minutes on this task.

Write about the following topic:

> *Today, the media portrays young people as lazy and disrespectful.*
>
> *Do you think this true? Are young people today worse than their parents, or does every new generation get criticized by older people?*

Give reasons for your answer and include any relevant examples from your own knowledge or experience.

Write at least 250 words.

PRACTICE TEST 3 - SPEAKING

▶ **PART 1:** (4 – 5 minutes) Introduction and (getting to know you) interview

Examiner: Good morning. My name's ....
And your name is...? And you're from... ?
Can I see your passport please? Thank you.

- *Did you go to school in [your present country]... ?*
- *What were your favourite subjects at school?*
- *Did you learn a language at school?*
- *How do you keep fit?*
- *Do you prefer to be indoors or outdoors?*
- *Do you like reading?*
- *What sort of books do you like to read?*

Thank you.

▶ **PART 2:** (3 – 4 minutes) Individual long turn (monologue)

Examiner: Now I'm going to give you a card with some information about **INFLUENTIAL PEOPLE**.
You will have one minute to read the card and then I'd like you to talk about **INFLUENTIAL PEOPLE** for one or two minutes. You can make some notes to help you if you wish. All right?

> **Describe a person who has had a great influence on your life.**
>
> **You should say:**
>
> **who the person is**
>
> **why the person has had such an influence on your life**
>
> **how you know the person**
>
> **...and explain how you feel about the person.**

Examiner: Would you like to start now?

You give your talk and after 1 or 2 minutes the examiner will ask you a question or two.

- *Are there any other people who have had an influence on your life?*
- *Do you think you would be a good influence on people?*

Thank you.

▶ **PART 3:** (4 – 5 minutes) Two-way discussion (more abstract conversation)

Examiner: Now I'd like to ask you a few more questions.

- *Who are you influenced by more – film stars or sports stars?*
- *What qualities does an influential person have?*
- *Do you think young people of today are too easily influenced?*
- *What sorts of things do young people get influenced by?*

Thank you very much.
That's the end of the speaking test. Goodbye.

PRACTICE TEST 4 - LISTENING

SECTION 1:   QUESTIONS 1 – 10

Listen to two students talking about libraries in Australia.

Questions 1 – 2

*Choose the correct letter from **A – D** for each answer.*

> **Example:**   Why is Yumi worried?
>
> **A**   She's a new student.
> **B**   She doesn't know very much about libraries.
> **C**   She hasn't used a library much.
> **D**   She has a lot of assignments.
>
> ANSWER: **B**

1   Who advised Yumi to join the local library?

   A   her tutor
   B   Mary Ann's tutor
   C   the librarian
   D   Mary Ann and Yumi's flatmate

2   What items cannot be borrowed from the local library?

   A   **B**   **C**   **D**

Questions 3 – 4

*Choose the correct letter from **A – C** for each answer.*

3   If Yumi returns a book two days after the loan period has ended,

   A   she will have to pay a fine.
   B   she will have to pay 10 cents.
   C   it won't cost her anything.

4   Why hasn't Yumi been to the university library yet?

   A   She couldn't attend the orientation activities.
   B   She has been sick all week.
   C   She had to go to her lecture.

Questions 5 – 9

Label the map of the library below.
Choose the correct letter from **A – E**
for each answer.

E

Quiet Study Area

A

5 Returns Box ....

6 Library Computers ....

7 Monograph Collection ....

8 Reference Section ....

9 Advisors' Desk ....

D

B

Photocopiers

Circulations Desk

C

Main
Entrance

Question 10

Complete the sentence below.
Use **NO MORE THAN THREE WORDS** for your answer.

10 Yumi should borrow Recommended Texts from the library as soon as possible

because ....

SECTION 2:   QUESTIONS 11 – 20

Questions 11 – 16

Complete the notes below.
Use **NO MORE THAN THREE WORDS OR A NUMBER** for each answer.

<u>INTERNATIONAL DRIVING LICENSES</u>

FACTS:
- have been used **(11)** ....
- drivers do not have to speak the native tongue of the country they are visiting
- drivers must be at least 18 years of age
- drivers must hold a driving license in their home country

SPECIFICATIONS OF BOOKLET:

Size of license: 10.8 x   **(12)** .... cm

Number of pages: 17

Colour of inside pages: **(13)** ....

Has a photograph of the driver and their **(14)** ....

Available from authorized travel agencies and the **(15)** ....

Cost of 3 year license: **(16)** ....

Questions 17 – 20

Complete the summary of International Driving Licenses below.
*Use **NO MORE THAN THREE WORDS** for each answer.*

International Driving Licenses cannot be used in the **(17)** .... They may only be used in some

countries for **(18)** .... Drivers using International Driving Licenses must obey the **(19)** ....

of the country that they are driving in. The driver must be responsible for learning the rules of the host

country, because if they break the rules, they may be **(20)** ....

SECTION 3:   QUESTIONS 21 – 30

Questions 21 – 24

Complete the chart below.
*Match the advantages of joining a learning circle (**I – VI**) to the person.*

NOTE: there are more advantages listed than you will need.

Reasons for joining a learning circle given by:

Economics tutor   **(21)** ....

Hamish   **(22)** ....

(23) ....

Anita   **(24)** ....

Advantages of a learning circle

I   commits to other students with a shared purpose
II   can provide motivation to study
III   commits time to study
IV   can provide help with understanding subject material
V   can provide support for other students
VI   saves the cost of an expensive tutor

Questions 25 – 27

Choose the correct letter from A – C for each answer.

25 The purpose of studying past exam papers is to

    A do well in the end of term exam.
    B contribute to the learning circle.
    C compare answers of past papers with other students.

26 By doing mock tutorials in the learning circle, the students hope to

    A practise by themselves first.
    B help each other by giving practical advice.
    C gain self-confidence.

27 Hamish advises Anita to

    A make a list of objectives for the first learning circle.
    B commit to the learning circle and then get a tutor.
    C trial the learning circle first.

Question 28

Choose the correct letter from A – D.

28 When was/is the first learning circle study session?

    A last week
    B next week
    C Thursday, 6th August
    D this evening

Questions 29 – 30

Choose TWO letters from A – E.

29 & 30 Which two activities are most likely to be discussed at the next learning circle?

    A past exam papers
    B learning styles
    C lecture notes
    D reading comprehension
    E how to re-write lecture notes

SECTION 4: QUESTIONS 31 – 40

Questions 31 – 32

Complete the notes below.
Use NO MORE THAN THREE WORDS for each answer.

Reasons given for speaker adopting wind-generating power:

- lives on a windy farm
- electricity not supplied by (31) ....
- diesel and petrol generators' lack of efficiency and excessive (32) ....

Questions 33 – 36

Complete the time-line below.
*Use **NO MORE THAN THREE WORDS OR A NUMBER** for each answer.*

1975	-	speaker bought farm
	-	relied on diesel and petrol generators
Late 1975	-	Hybrid system installed
	-	successful even in **(33)** ....
(34)	-	stopped operating **(35)** .... and relied solely on wind generator
	-	imported four wind generators from the **(36)** .... who now supply 50% of world's wind turbines
Last year	-	bought 600-kilowatt wind turbine

Questions 37 – 39

Look at the picture of wind turbines below and complete the following information in the table below.

Details of a 600-kilowatt wind turbine given by the speaker	
(37)	46 metres
Diameter of rotors:	43.5 metres
Power output:	**(38)** .... kilowatt hours per year
Life expectancy:	20 years
Maintenance:	**(39)** .... a year

Question 40

Complete the sentence below.
*Use **NO MORE THAN THREE WORDS** for your answer.*

40 Possible sources of future income for the speaker include:

- tourists visiting the 'wind farm'.
- .... to State Electricity Commission.

PRACTICE TEST 4 - READING

PART 1

*First, read the information below and answer **Questions 1 – 6**.*

The Essential Beauty Guide

B Vitamins	These are found in wholegrains and wheatgerm and will help to nourish your whole body. Including these vitamins in your diet will give you energy and an overall feeling of well-being, so you are less likely to get sick.
Vitamin A	It protects the skin against redness and inflammation caused by skin rashes. Try to eat plenty of dark orange (carrots, sweet potato) and dark green (broccoli and spinach) vegetables every day.
Vitamin C	This vitamin helps to build collagen, the "glue" that holds the body's cells together. It also promotes clear, healthy eyes. Include raw fruits and vegetables especially blueberries, kiwi fruit, citrus fruits, red capsicum and broccoli in your diet.
Zinc	It is essential for wound healing and new skin growth. It is found in lean beef, liver, seafood, wholegrains, pulses, milk and eggs.
Vitamin E	It guards the skin against premature ageing. Eat lots of sunflower seeds and raw nuts such as walnuts, pecans and almonds as snacks.
Calcium	This adds moisture and lustre to hair and nails. The best sources of calcium are healthy oils including canola and olive oil. You should also try to eat lots of almonds, walnuts and seeds.
Potassium	This essential product hydrates the skin and regulates normal function of the oil glands keeping the skin moist and supple, not thin and dry. It is found mostly in bananas.

Questions 1 – 6

*Answer the questions below using **NO MORE THAN THREE WORDS** for each answer.*

Write your answers in boxes 1 – 6 on your Answer Sheet.

What vitamins or minerals should you take if you have:

1   dry, flaky skin? ....

2   a cut that won't heal? ....

3   dry, thin hair? ....

4   poor general health and are often ill? ....

5   a face that looks older than your age? ....

6   a skin rash? ....

*Now read the passage below and answer **Questions 7 – 13**.*

GL ALLURA FROST FREE REFRIGERATOR

Welcome to Allura, the latest in GL's series of frost-free refrigerators. With its curved edges and smooth lines, it'll bring grace and style to contemporary kitchens.

COOLING SYSTEM
You'll never have to defrost the freezer manually again. The patented cooling system circulates cold air throughout the freezer compartments, so ice never forms anywhere on the sides. Each shelf is designed with its own cold air outlet so you can be sure that your food and drink will taste its best and last longer. Wine and beer are kept at an ideal temperature by placing them in the special chilled drinks section in the centre of the fridge section.

ENERGY EFFICIENCY
The energy rating is the easiest method of comparing the energy efficiency of similar products. More stars equals greater energy and efficiency. So by owning a 5 star GL fridge, you'll save power and money compared to a less energy-efficient model. Over the life of the refrigerator that could equate to hundreds of pounds.

STORAGE
All trays slide out for easy cleaning. The see-through shelves are wide enough to store an array of food, and the chilled food crisper at the bottom of the fridge compartment keeps vegetables fresher for longer. The special bottle storage areas have grooves to hold all bottles and jars in place no matter what their size. Never again will you have to contend with bottles falling over and spilling when you open the door.

ADDITIONAL FEATURES
Additional features include an ice-cube maker halfway up the door of the freezer section, which with just one twist, sends ice-cubes falling into the tray below. It makes serving drinks at a party really easy, especially since the ice tray refreezes in less than 1 hour. The fast freeze section in the lowest section of the freezer ensures meat can be frozen quickly and hygienically.

WARRANTY
All GL refrigerators come with a 12-month warranty on parts and labour. In addition, send in your completed warranty form and a copy of your receipt within 28 days, and we will give you another 12 month warranty on parts - absolutely free.

Questions 7 – 8

*Choose the correct letter from **A– D** to answer the questions below and write it in boxes 7 – 8 on your Answer Sheet.*

7   The Allura series refrigerators

    A   have a unique cooling system.
    B   need to be defrosted once a year.
    C   are only suitable for large families.
    D   are more fuel efficient than other brands of fridges.

8   If your fridge breaks down 400 days after you bought it, you

    A   will be able to have it fixed at no charge.
    B   will have to pay for the replacement parts.
    C   need to send off a copy of your receipt to get the replacement parts free.
    D   may be covered for some of the repairs.

Questions 9 – 13

Look at the following items (**Questions 9 – 13**) and the positions in the refrigerator below.

Match each item with its correct position in the refrigerator.

Write the correct letter **A – H** in boxes 9 – 13 on your Answer Sheet.

		Answer
Example:	sausages	.....**B**....
9	champagne for a party	....
10	carrots and cabbage	....
11	ice for the party	....
12	chicken to be cooked in the following week	....
13	a jar of mayonnaise	....

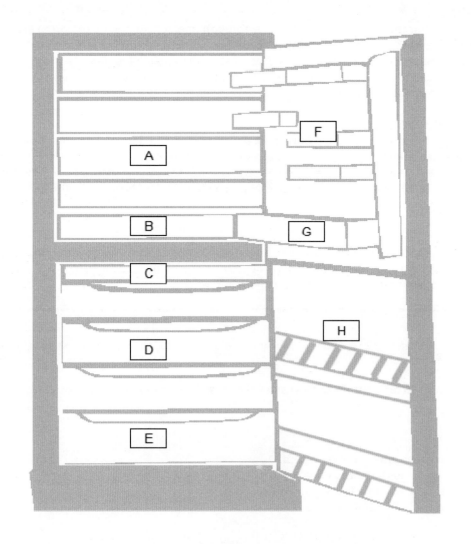

PART 2

Read the information below about a company's timesheet and answer **Questions 14 – 20**.

How to complete your timesheet

One of the main reasons for a delay in pay results from an incomplete or incorrect timesheet. In addition, if a timesheet is not filled out correctly, it may result in the company not correctly billing a client. The steps below show you how to complete your timesheet.

Before you start
Gather together your diary or notepad. This should contain details of any meetings or appointments you have had during that week. Although the cut off time for completing your timesheet for the previous week is Monday lunchtime, you may find it easier to write your hours in at the end of each day.

Make a note of the time you arrive and leave, and the breaks that you take. If you work more than five hours, you must take a break of at least thirty minutes and mark this on your timesheet.

Entering Your Employee Details
The first part of filling out your timesheet is the employee identification section. You will need to include your full name, your department, your employee identification number and your work phone number.

Note: when you have completed this section, you can save it for next time. However, you should always check it in case there has been a change in your details.

Entering Non-Billable Hours
There are two different types of hours to enter on your time sheet, billable and non-billable hours. When writing out the details for non-billable hours, you will need to include the codes for the various types of non-billable hours. For example, non-billable hours generally include things like working on bids for new projects, completing general administrative tasks, and attending training sessions or committee meetings. The full list of codes can be found on the intranet under timesheet codes.

Entering Billable Hours
In the billable hours section, you need to ensure that you include all the relevant details of work completed for clients. Remember to include the client code, a clear description of the work undertaken, and the number of hours – rounded off to the nearest fifteen minutes. It is imperative that you obtain the correct codes for any client before commencing work on any project. Speak to your project manager if you are not sure which code to use.

Entering Expenses
This step is optional – if you do not have any expenses, go to finalising a timesheet. Complete the details for any work-related expenses that you have incurred in this period. You must attach a tax invoice for each expense. This invoice should include the date and the business tax number of the company supplying the goods or services.

Finalising a Time Sheet
Before submitting your timesheet to your supervisor, you will need to total up the hours. If you have exceeded 40 hours in the week, you will need to seek approval from your manager before you can claim overtime. Once you are satisfied that the details are correct, sign and date the timesheet. It is recommended that you take a photocopy for your own records in case of a dispute.

Questions 14 – 20

Complete the sentences below with words taken from the reading passage.

Choose **NO MORE THAN TWO WORDS** *for each answer. Write your answers in boxes 14 – 20 on your Answer Sheet.*

14 Make sure you submit your timesheet by ....

15 Don't forget to write down any .... you have in the day.

16 By choosing to .... your details, you can avoid having to enter them each time.

17 Timesheeting codes for courses can be obtained from the ....

18 A .... receipt is required to claim any money spent on business items.

19 Provided you .... from the manager, you may claim overtime.

20 You are strongly advised to .... your timesheet prior to submitting it.

Questions 21 – 27

*Read the information below to answer **Questions 21 – 27**.*

Careers at *Northern Outlets*

What *Northern Outlets* will do for you as an employee!

A. Size doesn't matter when it comes to motivation! Every business needs it and, in fact, at *Northern Outlets* we believe that the success of our business relies on having a team of motivated, hard-working employees. Employees who lose motivation become less productive and less creative, so their job performance is affected. This can be seen over a period of years as the performance of former hard-working employees declines or as the productivity of long-term employees fails to increase.

B. Prior to your commencement at *Northern Outlets*, we will ask you about your expectations and career goals because we want you to feel part of the team immediately. We share the history of our business with all new employees, as well as our own vision for the future, in a very thorough welcome program. As a new employee, your orientation and introduction to *Northern Outlets* will provide you with a strong base to help motivate you to achieve from day one.

C. Our aim is to build a positive company environment where all employees feel worthwhile and valued. We encourage our staff to talk to their managers when they have questions, suggestions or concerns. It is our belief that a happy office is a productive office and so *Northern Outlets* tries hard to make you feel happy.

D. One way in which we do this is to work *with* you to develop a career strategy that takes into consideration your current skills *and* your future goals. *Northern Outlets* believes that if you are excited about your own future possibilities, you will become more engaged in your present work.

E. *Northern Outlets* also assists its employees to improve their professional skills by providing on-the-job training. Attendance at industry-related workshops and seminars is optional but encouraged by management. We pay for adult education classes too, so make sure that you sign up!

F. Awards and other incentives, such as a gift certificate or a salary bonus, are given to you when you perform well. *Northern Outlets* rewards its employees for hard work. You will be able to see in very practical ways that your contribution is appreciated by management.

G. *Northern Outlets* prides itself on keeping all of the promises we make to our employees. We recognise that trust is an important element to company morale, and confidently state, in writing, that we will deliver everything we say in our recruitment and employment packages.

H. It is our aim at *Northern Outlets* to motivate you and increase your confidence by assigning you tasks that we know you will be good at. We know that your success will give you the self-confidence to try new things and strive to achieve in different aspects of your life.

I. So, in conclusion, it is demonstrably clear why *Northern Outlets* is such a successful business. With 10 operating divisions around Australia, we have become known for service that is reliable in a modern world where many companies that deliver a similar service have lost credibility. And one significant reason for this reliability can be summed up in three words: *Northern Outlets* employees.

Questions 21 – 27

The reading passage has nine paragraphs labelled **A – I**.

Which paragraphs contain the following information?

NOTE: there are more paragraphs than questions, and you may use a letter once only.

Write the correct letter **A – I** *in boxes 21 – 27 on your Answer Sheet.*

		Answer
21	An account of activities on your first day of work	....
22	A recommendation that *Northern Outlets* considers useful	....
23	An explanation of the significance of enthusiastic employees	....
24	A comparison between *Northern Outlets* and other businesses	....
25	An analysis of a principle that the company is based on	....
26	A reason for assisting workers with job growth plans	....
27	A description of how to have a contented workplace	....

PART 3

Questions 28 – 40 are based on the reading passage below.

A MATTER OF LIFE AND DEATH   cancer   cancer   cancer

Cancer is the second leading cause of death in the United States, but the risk of developing most types of cancer can be reduced by changes in a person's lifestyle, for example, by quitting smoking and having a healthy diet.

The body is made up of many different types of cells which grow, divide and produce more cells than are needed to keep the body healthy and functioning properly. During the early years of a person's life, normal cells divide more rapidly until the person becomes an adult. After that, cells in most parts of the body divide to replace worn-out or dying cells and to repair injuries. Sometimes, however, the process goes inexplicably awry - cells keep dividing when new cells are not needed. Cancer cells are different from normal cells because instead of dying, they outlive normal cells and continue to form new abnormal cells. The mass of extra cells that come about due to chaotic processes forms a tumour or growth. Benign tumours are not cancer and do not represent a threat to health. Malignant tumours are, however, life-threatening – they are abnormal and divide without control or order, destroying the tissue around them. Cancer cells can also break away from a malignant tumour and enter the bloodstream or lymphatic system (the tissues and organs that produce, store, and carry white blood cells that fight infection and other diseases). This is called metastasis and is the way in which the original (primary) tumour goes on to form new (secondary) tumours in other parts of the body. When cells from a cancer like lung cancer spread to another organ like the liver, the cancer is still called lung cancer, not liver cancer.

There are many different types of cancer – two of the most common being lung cancer and skin cancer or melanoma.

Researchers have discovered several causes of lung cancer, most of which are directly related to the use of, or exposure to certain substances. For example, tobacco in cigarettes, cigars and pipes contains harmful carcinogens which actively damage the cells in the lungs and over time become cancerous. Radon is an invisible, odourless and tasteless radioactive gas that can cause damage to lungs leading possibly to lung cancer. Asbestos is the name of a group of minerals that occur naturally as fibres and are used in certain industries. When asbestos particles are inhaled, they can lodge in the lungs, damaging cells and increasing the risk of lung cancer.

Because lung cancer is difficult to diagnose, it is important to be aware of common signs and symptoms which may include localised pain and respiratory problems such as a persistent cough and shortness of breath.

Treatment depends on a number of factors, including the type of lung cancer, the size, location and extent of the tumour, and the general health of the patient. Many different treatments and combinations of treatments may be used to control lung cancer and/or to improve quality of life. Treatment options include surgery, chemotherapy, radiation therapy and PDT, which is a kind of laser therapy.

Melanoma is also a very common cancer. No one knows its exact cause, but research has shown that certain variables may be instrumental in causing malignant melanomas. Firstly, certain pigmentary traits are possibly the most important of the cancer indicators: light skinned individuals are shown to be at greatest risk while those with darker complexions are protected by their melanin pigmentation. In addition, skin cancer has also been associated in some studies with light coloured or reddish hair, light coloured eyes and the presence of freckling. In addition to, and separate from the physical factors discussed, hereditary factors such as the existence of a family history of skin cancer can significantly increase an individual's chances of developing the disease, especially if one or more of the other risk variables are present. Finally, the popularity of sunbathing and the current trend in outdoor activities over the last few decades are also considered to be high behavioural risk factors.

The first sign of melanoma is a change in the size, shape, colour and feel of an existing mole. Melanoma may also appear as a new mole – it will be black, abnormal and ugly-looking. There are a variety of treatment options for patients, including surgery, chemotherapy, biological therapy and radiation therapy. Patients may also benefit from a combination of treatments.

Through research, doctors are exploring new and possibly more effective ways to treat cancer. A recent safety trial will test a new treatment strategy that aims to boost the body's immune system to attack any remaining cancerous cells after surgical removal of a tumour. Under the trial, blood will be taken from each patient and processed in the lab to boost the dendritic cells, and then exposed to the radiated tumour cells removed during surgery. The modified blood cells will then be injected back into each individual patient as a vaccine. Dendritic cells – a subpopulation of white blood cells – are known triggers for the immune system and are being used in Australian and international research into treatments for melanomas and lung cancer.

Questions 28 – 32

*Using information from the reading passage, write if the statements (**Questions 28 – 32**) below are*

TRUE	*if the statement agrees with the information*
FALSE	*if the statement contradicts the information*
NOT GIVEN	*if there is no information on this.*

Write your answers in boxes 28 – 32 on your Answer Sheet.

Answer

28   A poor diet increases the risk of developing cancer.   ....

29   Cell division occurs throughout a person's life.   ....

30   Rapid cell division signals the beginning of cancer.   ....

31   Blood can carry cancer cells to other parts of the body.   ....

32   The incidence of lung cancer and skin cancer is increasing.   ....

Questions 33 – 38

Complete the table below with words taken from the reading passage.

Use **NO MORE THAN THREE WORDS** for each answer.

Write your answers in boxes 33 – 38 on your Answer Sheet.

Cancer	Risk Factors	Symptoms	Treatment Options
Lung	- dangerous substances	- localised pain	- surgery
	- **(33)**	- **(36)**	- chemotherapy
	- radon		- radiation therapy
	- asbestos		- PDT/laser therapy
Melanoma	■ *Physical:*	- **(37)**	- surgery
	- light skin	- new moles	- chemotherapy
	- reddish hair		- biological therapy
	- light-coloured eyes		- radiation
	- freckling		- **(38)** ....
	■ **(34)** .... :		
	- family history		
	■ **(35)** .... :		
	- popularity of sunbathing		
	- current trend for outdoor activities		

Questions 39 – 40

Choose the correct letter from **A – D** to answer the questions below. Write the answers in boxes 39 – 40 on your Answer Sheet.

39 The aim of cancer research is to

    A boost the immune system of cancer patients.

    B find improved ways of fighting cancer.

    C create treatments for melanomas and lung cancer in Australia and internationally.

    D develop a vaccine for individual patients.

40 The purpose of the text is to

    A inform doctors.

    B warn people about lung and skin cancer.

    C compare lung and skin cancer.

    D discuss cancer.

PRACTICE TEST 4 - WRITING

WRITING TASK 1

You should spend about 20 minutes on this task.

> *A friend's son is starting to learn English as a Second Language next semester. Your friend has asked you to offer some advice to his son about studying a foreign language.*
>
> *Write a letter to your friend's son. In your letter*
>
> - *make some suggestions based on your own experiences of learning a second language*
> - *offer advice about how to get the most out of studying another language*
> - *mention some of the benefits and difficulties involved.*

Write at least 150 words.

You do **NOT** need to write any addresses.

Begin your letter as follows:

Dear Sir or Madam,

WRITING TASK 2

You should spend about 40 minutes on this task.

Write about the following topic:

> *The difference between the rich and poor in the world seems to be getting larger.*
>
> *What do you think are the causes of this? What, in your opinion, should be done to stop this from happening?*

Give reasons for your answer and include any relevant examples from your own knowledge or experience.

Write at least 250 words.

PRACTICE TEST 4 - SPEAKING

▶ **PART 1:** (4 – 5 minutes) Introduction and (getting to know you) interview

Examiner: Good morning. My name's ....
And your name is...? And you're from... ?
Can I see your passport please? Thank you.

- *What do you like about living in [your present country]... ?*
- *Can you tell me about your last holiday?*
- *Where would you like to travel to in the future?*
- *What do you plan to do in the future?*
- *How do you spend your free time?*
- *Do you like to relax with others or by yourself?*
- *Tell me about your best friend.*

Thank you.

▶ **PART 2:** (3 – 4 minutes) Individual long turn (monologue)

Examiner: Now I'm going to give you a card with some information about **EDUCATION**. You will have one minute to read the card and then I'd like you to talk about **EDUCATION** for one or two minutes. You can make some notes to help you if you wish. All right?

Describe your school life.

You should say:

how long your school day was

what subjects you studied

who your favourite teachers were

...and explain whether or not you think that your education was useful.

Examiner: Would you like to start now?

You give your talk and after 1 or 2 minutes the examiner will ask you a question or two.

- *Did you find studying English easy at school?*
- *Is there any subject that you wish you could have studied?*

Thank you.

▶ **PART 3:** (4 – 5 minutes) Two-way discussion (more abstract conversation)

Examiner: Now I'd like to ask you a few more questions.

- *School years are the best years of your life. Do you agree with this?*
- *What qualities do you think a good teacher needs to have?*
- *Do you think that school gives you the skills to succeed in life?*
- *What other subjects do you think schools should teach to prepare students for life?*

Thank you very much.
That's the end of the speaking test. Goodbye.

ANSWER KEYS

NB: • words in brackets are optional
    • alternative answers are separated with a stroke (/)
    • both British and American spellings are acceptable

• the omission of initial capitals is generally not penalised, but candidates are advised to capitalise the first letter of proper nouns (especially people's names)

• IELTS will accept any reasonable variation of an answer that requires a date, including abbreviations e.g. 9 September, 9 Sept., 9th Sept, 09.09

PRACTICE TEST 1:

Listening

1	£203	21	A
2	17	22	B
3	no	23	A
4	under 26 / less than 26	24	E OR E/A
5	locals / local people	25	C
6	satisfied / OK	26	D OR D/C
7	(British) students	27	Early Childhood
8	(too) many / big	28	the differences / how they differ
9	careful	29	not learned / innate
10	the culture / the food	30	in person
11	International Student Advisor	31	higher
12	learning / study groups	32	exam performance / results
13	Student IT Department	33	sleep / sleeping / sleeplessness
14	Housing Officer / Accommodation Officer	34	controlled
15	International Department	35	thought / thinking
16	personal and/or financial	36	organised
17	B	37	vary / change / be different
18	D	38	marks / weighting
19	E	39	relaxed
20	C	40	(effective) study skills

23/24 A E OR E A
25/26 C D OR D C

Reading

1	D	28	feedback
2	C	29	strategies
3	A	30	evaluate
4	B		
5	A	31	1592
6	D	32	1627
7	any/every Monday	33	son/Aurangzeb overthrew father/Jahan
8	business and academic	34	1666
9	join a class / try it first / try a class	35	love/cherish sons OR visit the/her tomb
10	over 20	36	visit the/her tomb OR love/cherish sons
11	tours and excursions	37	D
12	(at the) website / (on the) Internet	38	C
13	B	39	B
14	D	40	B
15	F		
16	A		
17	G		
18	C		
19	YES		
20	YES		
21	NOT GIVEN		
22	NO		
23	NO		
24	NOT GIVEN		
25	less rigid		
26	meetings		
27	aware		

Answers to exercise on page 125:

1 non-tertiary 2 vocabulary 3 appropriate
4 prepare 5 interviews 6 focus 7 analyse 8 valid

PRACTICE TEST 1 continued:

Writing

Example answers are given for Practice Test 1 in this book. Model answers for Test 2, 3 and 4 can be found in the accompanying Study Guide to the 404 Essential Tests for IELTS.

Task 1

Dear Sir or Madam,

RE: Campsite Enquiry

I have been looking with interest at your advertisement in The Holidaymaker section of "The Daily News" and I am particularly interested in your Sundancer campsite in northern New South Wales.

I would like to know whether there are any vacancies at the Sundancer campsite at the start of August for one week, arriving Tuesday 1st and departing Monday 7th August. Also, would you please let me know how much it will cost for my friend and me to stay for the week and whether you charge any extra for the campsites which are located closer to the beach? We will be camping in a tent, and do not require a site with power. In addition, I would also be grateful if you could send me information about the facilities you offer at the campsite, and whether there is any extra cost for using any of these facilities.

I would appreciate a reply as soon as possible, as my friend and I would like to begin planning our holiday.

Yours sincerely,

Mary Jane Smythe

(181 words)

Task 2

Movies tend to have a very large influence on young people who are influenced both by what they see and hear. Because this is the case, it is true that car chases in action movies tend to lead to an increase in the number of car accidents among young drivers because they try to copy what they have seen in the films. They drive too fast and take unnecessary risks and the difficulty is that most young people lack the skills and experience to do this.

There are a variety of ways in which young people can be encouraged to practise safer driving habits. Firstly, the Government should launch a safe driving campaign to convey the fact that driving safely is not uncool. In effect, it should be cool to stay alive and healthy! Secondly, every movie should make it clear that dangerous car chases are undertaken only in strict safety conditions with experienced drivers, and often special movie-making tricks are used to enhance the action. Thirdly, young people should be forced to take safe driving courses every year for the first five years that they have their driver's licence. In this way, they are forced to perfect their driving skills or their licence will be taken away.

Finally, as part of this course, young drivers should go to hospitals and witness the effects of poor or dangerous driving on other people. When they see hospitalised people whose lives have been destroyed due to stupid risk-taking, they will surely change their minds about whether it is cool to copy action heroes and drive fast.

(264 words)

PRACTICE TEST 2:

Listening

1	0278804	21	C
2	2, 5 / 5, 2 / May 2nd / 2nd May	22	B
3	17 Rocksford	23	A
4	5 p.m.	24	A
5	doorbell	25	C
6	teacher	26	G
7	pay / salary / money	27	D
8	no / break from	28	B
9	(long) summer holiday	29	A
10	by himself / by myself / alone / on his own	30	F

11	A	31	beginning and completion/ending/end
12	A	32	a schedule
13	B	33	four stages
14	B ‖ OR D	34	developing a plan / planning a project
15	D ‖ OR B	35	realistically
16	nearest police station	36	help / advice (from others / other people)
17	cross street / intersection	37	Gant Chart
18	café / (nearest) shop	38	standard of delivery
19	detailed / full description	39	(the) Quality Assurance
20	canceling them	40	(the / your / this week's) tutorials

Reading

1	drip-tray	28	B
2	fuel source	29	A
3	small baskets / roasting trays	30	C
4	A	31	D
5	C	32	items / triggers / things
6	C	33	interest in asthma
7	B	34	(asthma) medication
8	C	35	Asthma Action Plan
9	B	36	E
10	D	37	F
11	B	38	B
12	C	39	D
13	A	40	F

14	TRUE
15	NOT GIVEN
16	TRUE
17	FALSE
18	NOT GIVEN
19	TRUE
20	FALSE
21	online
22	store location
23	(general) profile
24	job alert
25	Group Gathering
26	customer service
27	personal references

Writing

Example answers are given for Practice Test 1 in this book. Model answers for Test 2, 3 and 4 can be found in the accompanying Study Guide to the 404 Essential Tests for IELTS.

PRACTICE TEST 3:

Listening

1	A	21	C
2	B	22	329,758
3	I Block	23	about/over/more than 3 million
4	C Block	24	75% / ¾ of population
5	Student Canteen	25	friendly
6	have an interview / be interviewed	26	continuing to grow / growing
7	2 p.m. / 2 o'clock / 2:00 / 2.00	27	US, Japan
8	Pastel	28	tourism / number of tourists
9	0412 987 35	29	education and technology
10	BI 690011	30	eastern and western
11	C	31	thousands of years
12	C	32	has (been) grown
13	A	33	C ‖ OR E
14	9 Sept / 9th September	34	E C
15	Music / opera	35	C ‖ OR E
16	Festival Club	36	E C
17	14 Sept / 14th September	37	dried fruit(s)
18	Performing Arts Centre	38	seaweed
19	City Football Club	39	cereals
20	Under the Stars	40	www.vegsoc.org

Reading

1	TRUE	28	FALSE
2	FALSE	29	NOT GIVEN
3	TRUE	30	NOT GIVEN
4	FALSE	31	TRUE
5	FALSE	32	NOT GIVEN
6	NOT GIVEN	33	TRUE
7	UP Choir Trials	34	banned / not allowed / forbidden
8	Vivaldi Concert	35	(GM) ingredients
9	Uniclean Awareness Day	36	(big) biotech companies
10	UP Storewide Sale	37	exports / international trade
11	$40 / full price	38	blindness
12	fireworks and dance	39	pesticides / insecticides
13	School Music Concert	40	proteins
14	sold		
15	(office) supplies / goods		
16	performance		
17	price and quality		
18	environment		
19	manufacturing scraps		
20	(stationery) catalogues		
21	recycled content		
22	III		
23	VIII		
24	V		
25	II		
26	I		
27	IX		

Writing

Example answers are given for Practice Test 1 in this book. Model answers for Test 2, 3 and 4 can be found in the accompanying Study Guide to the 404 Essential Tests for IELTS.

PRACTICE TEST 4:

Listening

1	D	21	III	
2	D	22	II or VI	
3	A	23	VI or II	
4	A	24	IV	
5	C	25	A	
6	B	26	C	
7	A	27	C	
8	E	28	B	
9	D	29	B or C	

10	they are popular / of their popularity	30	C or B
11	since 1949	31	the state / the government / the grid
12	15.25	32	noise
13	white	33	moderately windy sites / less windy sites
14	signature	34	1984
15	Internet	35	diesel generator(s)
16	$80	36	Danes / Danish
17	home country / country of issue	37	Height / height
18	a limited time/period / a year	38	1,000,000 / 1 000 000 / 1 million
19	road rules	39	twice / two times
20	fined / penalized	40	selling power (back)

Reading

1	potassium	28	NOT GIVEN
2	zinc	29	TRUE
3	calcium	30	FALSE
4	B vitamins	31	TRUE
5	Vitamin E	32	NOT GIVEN
6	Vitamin A	33	tobacco / carcinogens
7	A	34	hereditary (factors)
8	D	35	behavioural (factors)
9	D	36	respiratory problems / (persistent) cough / shortness of breath
10	E	37	(old/existing) mole changes
11	F	38	combination (of treatments)
12	B	39	B
13	H	40	D

14	Monday lunchtime
15	break(s)
16	save
17	intranet
18	tax
19	seek approval
20	(photo)copy
21	B
22	E
23	A
24	I
25	G
26	D
27	C

Writing

Example answers are given for Practice Test 1 in this book. Model answers for Test 2, 3 and 4 can be found in the accompanying Study Guide to the 404 Essential Tests for IELTS.

LISTENING TESTS TAPESCRIPTS

TEST 1

SECTION 1

You will hear two students who have just returned to university after their summer vacation. Listen to Louise and Kerry talking about their vacation.

First, look at Questions 1 to 4.

[SHORT PAUSE]

You will see that there is an example already done for you. For this question only the conversation relating to the example will be played first.

Kerry	Hi Louise – how was your summer vacation?
Louise	Oh fantastic! I only got back from Europe yesterday.
Kerry	Wow! That sounds exciting.
Louise	Yes, it was. How was your holiday?
Kerry	Pretty quiet compared with yours. I just stayed around Cambridge…

Louise said that she had just got back from Europe yesterday, so the correct answer is EUROPE.

Now we shall begin. You should answer the questions as you listen because you will not hear the recording a second time.

Now listen carefully and answer Questions 1 to 4.

Kerry	Hi Louise – how was your summer vacation?
Louise	Oh fantastic! I only got back from Europe yesterday.
Kerry	Wow! That sounds exciting.
Louise	Yes, it was. How was your holiday?
Kerry	Pretty quiet compared with yours. I just stayed around Cambridge – but we're planning to go to Europe at the end of next term.
Louise	Oh you'll have a great time! I really recommend it. How are you going to get around?
Kerry	Well, we've thought about renting a car. Flying is far too expensive. What did you do?
Louise	We bought Eurail tickets and traveled around Europe by train.
Kerry	Was it expensive?
Louise	No, not really. It cost us £203 for a Eurailpass Youth Ticket.
Kerry	I've heard of Eurail – what did that include?
Louise	Well, you get unlimited train travel in and between seventeen European countries. It lasted for a month.
Kerry	Gee for £203 that sounds reasonable. Did you visit all of the seventeen places?
Louise	Yes, all except for Ireland. We couldn't really understand why Ireland was included on the pass but England wasn't.
Kerry	Yes, that seems a bit strange. Did it include the trip from London to Paris in the Channel Tunnel?
Louise	No, unfortunately we had to pay extra for that train but we did get a discounted fare because we're students.
Kerry	Were there any other restrictions on the tickets?
Louise	Well, if you want to pay more or less money you can choose another plan – there are 15 and 21 day plans or 2 and 3 month plans. The only restriction for the Youth Ticket is that you have to be under 26.
Kerry	That suits my friends and me. None of us are 26 yet. We went to school together.
Louise	Oh, you really have to do it. It's safe and easy and a great way see the countryside. The weather was fantastic and so were the people!
Kerry	It sounds great.

Louise and Kerry go on to talk about travelling by train in Europe. As you listen to the rest of the conversation , answer Questions 5 to 10.

Before the conversation continues, read Questions 5 to 10.

[SHORT PAUSE]

Kerry	What was the best part of your trip?
Louise	The trains really gave us the freedom to plan our own holiday. We went to lots of places which were out-of-the-way and met lots of local people – you know, small rural towns where trains are still an important form of transport.
Kerry	We'd like to meet the local people – did you do that easily?
Louise	Yes, the trains in Europe aren't like the commuter trains in London. People like to talk and have a chat on trains in Europe.
Kerry	That's nice.
Louise	Yes. The train times were OK as well. Sometimes we had to get up early to catch the trains which were crossing into another country but most of the time, we were satisfied with the timetables. Very punctual.
Kerry	Should we take an alarm clock?
Louise	Well, I would. Having an alarm clock made us sleep more comfortably. We knew that we'd wake up on time.
Kerry	And were the trains safe – did you travel at night?
Louise	Lots of students traveled at night because it saved having to pay for accommodation.
Kerry	I hadn't thought of that.
Louise	Well, lots of others have thought of it. We preferred to stay in local pubs or student hostels because you could mix with the locals. The night trains were filled with British students!
Kerry	It sounds as if you had a very positive experience. Is there anything you'd recommend we take or do?
Louise	Let me see – I can certainly tell you what not to take or do. Don't take much luggage. There just isn't very much room in the trains for big suitcases. A backpack or two small bags is better than one big bag. That way you can also get on and off the trains easily too.
Kerry	I'll remember that. My mother always says to pack one week before you go on vacation and then take half of it out the night before you leave.
Louise	That's good advice – especially when you're riding on cramped trains. The other thing is to be careful with your valuables. Lots of students had money and passports stolen – especially at night.
Kerry	Did you have anything stolen?
Louise	No but we met lots of people who did have things stolen. We all had money belts under our jackets.
Kerry	I'll have to buy one of those.
Louise	Yes, you should – or you can borrow mine if you like.
Kerry	Oh thanks – that'd be good.
Louise	The only other thing I'd advise you to do is to make sure you spend a reasonable amount of time in each country. We found that lots of students traveled too quickly and they didn't have enough time to meet the locals and enjoy the food and the culture.
Kerry	How long do you think you need in each country?
Louise	I can't say – it'll depend on who you meet and what you like to do and of course, the weather. It was so warm and sunny in some beach-side places that we stayed for four or five days. In other towns, if it was very quiet or boring, we just stayed overnight.
Kerry	I guess that's what's great about the train. You can come and go as you please.
Louise	Exactly – and it's cheaper and much more relaxing – not to mention safer – I don't think I could get used to driving on the right-hand-side of the road!

That is the end of Section 1. You now have ½ minute to check your answers.

Now turn to Section 2 of your Listening Question Booklet.

SECTION 2

You will hear Diane Kelly, the Admissions Officer at Central City University talking to a group of newly arrived international students.

As you listen to the first part of the talk answer Questions 11 to 16.

Before you listen, look at Questions 11 to 16.

[SHORT PAUSE]

DIANE KELLY:

For those of you I haven't met, my name is Diane Kelly, the International Admissions Officer at Central University.

Today, I'm here to explain some of the student support services which you might like to access during your courses. The first thing I'd like to make clear is that you are all entitled to this help – all you need to do is ask for it. You have full access to all of the regular university facilities here and additional services set up exclusively for international students.

These services are grouped under four main areas of responsibility – academic support, librarian services, administrative services and those provided by the student union.

The staff in Academic Support Services is qualified to assist you in course selection, content description and explanation of assessment criteria for individual subjects. We also have an International Student Advisor who is there to help students from non-English-speaking backgrounds. All of you have achieved the English requirements for entry to your particular courses but it is possible at some stage, that you will need language support. The International Student Advisor is there for that purpose. Be warned though – he is very busy at the end of semesters and he won't write your assignments for you!

If you need assistance with general study skills, the International Student Advisor will probably direct you to our library services staff. Library Services is made up of three departments – Research and Resource; Study Skills and the Student IT Department. The Study Skills Department is very active in promoting small learning and study groups. They will gladly help you to join one of these groups by matching your needs with other students.

After you get your student cards, the Student IT Department will arrange your email access and passwords for the university computers. You do need to have your student card first, so don't go there without it. Student cards are issued by Administration Officers in the Administration Student Services area.

A lot of you are in homestay at present, but if you want to move into more independent-style accommodation, see the Housing Officer at the Administration Building. Don't be too optimistic though – good, cheap accommodation close to the university is in high demand! It can be found but we advise you to see the Accommodation Officer early!

We also have a Student Employment Officer and of course the Homestay Officer, whom you would have met already.

The University Bookshop and most importantly, our International Department is in the Administration Building – so make sure that you come and see us if you have any questions about your passports or visas.

The Student Union is also very active and provides some great services. For example, if you have any personal or financial problems while you're here, the student union offers a Student Counselling Service. You will need to make appointments to see a counsellor. If you feel that you are not being treated fairly by another student or lecturer or university staff member, you might like to access the Equal Opportunity Service offered by them. They also run various social and sporting clubs and activity programs which I'd encourage you to sign up for.

Before the final part of the talk, look at Questions 17 to 20.

[SHORT PAUSE]

Now you will hear the rest of the talk. Answer Questions 17 to 20.

Obviously, you'll need to know where these services are. We're currently in the Grand Hall. Now if you have a look on your campus map – ah, the Library Services are of course in the library which is over to my right – just between the Outdoor Sporting Facilities and Hawkins Student Car Park. The Student Union Building is also in that same direction – but it's in front of the Car Park. For those of you who'll be travelling by bus, the university bus-stop is just outside the library.

The Administration Building is over to my left – between the International Centre and the Post Office. Most of you have been to visit us already. Even though the Administration Staff look after the Bookshop, it's in the same building as the Post Office – just behind the Student Refectory. If you come to the Administration Building, we'll show you where it is anyway.

All of the academic staff are found in their particular faculty buildings which you'll get to know very well. The Career and International Student Advisors are in a small building behind the International Centre, in between the English and the Arts Block. It's really quite easy to find your way around the campus and most staff and students are more than willing to give you directions.

Now we're just going to have a short break with some tea and biscuits at the back of the hall. So, if you'd like to stand up and come down…

That is the end of Section 2. You now have ½ minute to check your answers.

Now turn to Section 3 of your Listening Question Booklet.

SECTION 3

In this section you will hear two students discussing the Early Childhood Tutorial they are going to present.

First, look at Questions 21 to 26.

[SHORT PAUSE]

Now listen to the first part of the discussion and answer Questions 21 to 26.

Marie	I don't suppose you've come up with an idea for our tutorial presentation, have you?
Rose	Well, as a matter of fact, I have – I thought we could talk about the obvious differences we see between the sexes as children grow up.
Marie	Do you mean the differences we see between males and females as a result of the way they are brought up?
Rose	No, I mean the differences that exist from birth.
Marie	That sounds like a lot of work Rose …
Rose	Not really – do you remember in our first Early Childhood lecture, we were given a list of differences which were observed in male and female babies and toddlers in the UK?
Marie	I wasn't here for the first two weeks of the semester remember? I had problems getting my passport.
Rose	Oh, that's right. Well, it was really fascinating. A group of behavioural scientists in England selected 100 children to observe over a very long period – 20 or 25 years. They were brought up in families who treated girls and boys in the same way – no special treatment for either of the sexes. They observed their play and their reactions to various situations – set up little tests I suppose.
Marie	How old were the children?
Rose	The first observations were carried out when the babies were only a few hours old – they concluded that girls were more sensitive to touch than boys at that early age!
Marie	How did they end up with that conclusion?

Rose	Well, the lecturer didn't go into detail – I think he just wanted to get our interest, you know, whet our appetite. There were lots of tests and observations done from soon after birth, right through to their early twenties. I thought we could investigate some of the case studies and then present the results in the tutorial.
Marie	That's a good idea Rose. It'll be interesting but it will also give us the chance to collect information for our end-of-term assignment as well.
Rose	It'll also be a good opportunity to check out the resources available in the library. I haven't had the chance to spend much time there yet, have you?
Marie	The last four weeks have just been so busy – and of course, I had to catch up on the two weeks that I missed – I haven't had the chance either. I've heard that the library research staff are really willing to help out.
Rose	Well, we can find out if that's true or not. We'll need to make an appointment to see them. Apparently they're in high demand.
Marie	We only have two weeks to prepare for this tutorial, so I think we should definitely start as soon as we can. Let's see the tutor this afternoon and tell him about our plan. If he agrees, we can get started on our research.
Rose	OK – I'll go and see the tutor. You can make a booking at the library.

Rose goes to the tutor's office to discuss the topic for their tutorial.

Before listening to the rest of the conversation, look at Questions 27 to 30.

[SHORT PAUSE]

Rose	Would it be possible to see Jim Clark – one of the Early Childhood tutors?
AA (Admin Assistant)	May I ask what it's about?
Rose	We have to get approval for our tutorial topics in EC101.
AA	Yes, I thought it might be about that. Unfortunately, Jim had to go to Sydney this week but he has given me some specific questions to ask about the tutorials.
Rose	Oh, we were hoping to get started on our research – we've only got two weeks.
AA	Don't worry – Jim's phoning in twice a day. If you give me the details, I can give you an answer by tomorrow morning.
Rose	That's great. We are planning to present some case studies that were undertaken by a group of…
AA	Hang on. I just need a few <u>short</u> details – let me see, I have to write down what the subject of the tutorial is.
Rose	OK – I guess the topic is gender and when the sexes start to act differently.
AA	So, is it about how male and female children are different? What can I write here, next to TOPIC?
Rose	Well, what about "How the sexes differ"?
AA	OK – I'll put that down as your topic. Jim also wants to know the aim of your tutorial.
Rose	Well, there are two aims I suppose. The first is to show <u>how</u> they differ. But the other point we want to make is that the differences are innate – not learned.
AA	To – show – that – differences – between – the – sexes – are – innate – not learned. Right – that's the hard part. Now I need to know the date, time and room of your tutorial.
Rose	It's in two weeks – let's see, that'll be Tuesday 26th at 11 a.m. We are in Room B1203.
AA	And do you need any A/V material?
Rose	What does AV mean?
AA	Audio-visual – you know, TV, video, tape-recorder, overhead projector – that kind of thing.
Rose	I hadn't thought of that – guess we'll need an overhead projector. We haven't really started planning our tutorial yet – we just wanted to get initial approval from Jim.
AA	Never mind – you can always cancel the projector if you don't need it. Jim will phone in the morning – do you want to come and see me then or I can phone you if you like.
Rose	I have a lecture from 8 to 10 tomorrow morning – so I'll drop by after it finishes.
AA	Right – I'll see you then.

That is the end of Section 3. You now have ½ minute to check your answers.

Now turn to Section 4 of your Listening Question Booklet.

SECTION 4

You will hear a lecture being given by a university professor to first year students about the examination period.

First, look at Questions 31 to 40.

[SHORT PAUSE]

Now listen to the lecture and answer Questions 31 to 40.

PROFESSOR:

Welcome to our Examinations Workshop – this is an annual event which we've found very helpful for first year students like yourselves and I hope that this year will be no exception.

By now you'll all have realized that studying at university is quite different to studying at school. Some of you might have been shocked at one time or another during the semester, when you received results for your assignments that weren't as high as you'd expected. I trust that you've spoken to your lecturers and tutors and sorted out those issues. The truth is that the transition from school to university can be a difficult one. The academic standards are higher and of course, there is considerably less supervision at university and it's incumbent on the students to follow their own study regime.

My aim today though is to help you to learn how to cope with the impending exam period by giving you some practical strategies to take with you into the exam.

We've all known students who've had a good understanding of the subject material yet failed exams or performed well-below expectations. Likewise, we've known students that have to all intents and purposes done very little work and passed with flying colours. Often these results can be put down to one thing – stress or a lack of it.

Don't underestimate the importance that stress plays in exam performance. With any exam, you should front up feeling confident, relaxed and organized. Rightly or wrongly, exams in effect, not only test your academic ability, they test your frame of mind and your ability to perform under pressure.

Stress has to be managed on two fronts – the physiological and the psychological. We all recognise that stress affects us physically – I'm sure you've all experienced an increased pulse, or sweaty hands or underarms, or shortness of breath when placed in a stressful situation. Sleeplessness can also be a problem around exam time. The most effective way to manage these physiological reactions is through controlled breathing – which we'll practise later. By controlling or regulating your breathing, you'll find that you can put yourself rather effectively into a relaxed state.

Psychologically, stress affects the way you think. For an exam you need to think rationally and this is why you need to be confident and organized before walking into the exam. Continuing to think rationally after you read an exam paper which you know nothing about is very hard to do. But if you are organized and you've put in the time needed to learn the subject material, you will have the self-control you need to think rationally. Stress can make you panic – the worst thing you can do in an exam. Look at the question calmly and rationally dissect the question. And let's face it, even if you haven't prepared well enough, you'll still need to think rationally in order to do your best under those very trying circumstances!

Just while I think of it, this is probably a good time to tell you a piece of advice that I give first year students that come to see me. Don't rely on what other students tell you about the time they allocate to study. The reports we have had over the years have been ridiculously overestimated <u>and</u> underestimated. Follow your own study regime and don't listen to others. We're all different, so it stands to reason that the time we need to allocate to study will be different! Generally speaking, for every hour of lectures you attend, you will need another hour of follow-up or research work if you want to achieve good grades.

Right – so where was I? We have to learn how to control our breathing and we need to have enough confidence in our ability to be able to think rationally.

Time Management is another important factor that can make or break you in an exam situation. After you have gone through the breathing exercises which you'll be familiar with, read over the entire exam noting the different marks and weighting of questions. Only after you have done this can you allocate your own time to each question. If I had a dollar for every time a student has told me that they didn't do as well in an exam as they'd hoped, because they'd run out of time I'd be rich! If you can manage your time properly in an exam, you will reduce the amount of pressure that you're under.

Anyway, note the different questions and their marks and allocate your time accordingly – as I said. Then, answer the questions that you know first. This serves to relax you further and gives you the confidence you might need to tackle the more difficult questions. However, don't spend too much time on the easy questions either – always be mindful of the time restraint and the marks that are assigned to the question.

In summary, to do well in an exam, you not only need the academic ability – you need to be in a relaxed state of mind with the ability to think clearly enough under pressure, to allocate suitable time frames to questions. If you can equip yourself with these skills and train yourself to observe time management, exam success is almost guaranteed.

We'll be holding a study skills workshop next week in the Language & Learning Centre to deal with ways in which you can study effectively for exams. You are all welcome of course.

Right, now are you ready to learn some controlled breathing exercises?

That is the end of Section 4 and the end of the Listening Test. You now have ½ minute to check your answers.

[PAUSE]

You now have 10 minutes to transfer your answers to your Answer Booklet.

TEST 2

SECTION 1

You will hear an external student making an appointment with a receptionist to see a counsellor at Grisham College.

First, look at Questions 1 to 5.

[SHORT PAUSE]

You will see that there is an example already done for you. For this question only the conversation relating to the example will be played first.

Jack	I'd like to make an appointment to see a student counsellor.
Receptionist	Yes, certainly. Are you a student at the college?
Jack	Yes – I'm studying Linguistics, 2ⁿᵈ year.
Receptionist	Right. I'll just get a few details.

Jack said that he is in his second year which means he is a current student – so B is the correct answer.

Now we shall begin. You should answer the questions as you listen because you will not hear the recording a second time.

Now listen carefully and answer Questions 1 to 5.

Jack	I'd like to make an appointment to see a student counsellor.
Receptionist	Yes, certainly. Are you a student at the college?
Jack	Yes – I'm studying Linguistics, 2ⁿᵈ year.
Receptionist	Right. I'll just get a few details. What's your student number?
Jack	0278804.
Receptionist	0 – 2 – 7 – double 8 – 0 – 4 … and there should be three letters on the end of that?
Jack	Oh yes, EXT – I guess that means external.
Receptionist	Yes, that's right. Jack Larassy – is that right?
Jack	Yes, that's me.
Receptionist	What's your date of birth Jack?
Jack	2ⁿᵈ May 1979.
Receptionist	Are you still living in Maldon?
Jack	No – I moved to Chelmsford last week actually.
Receptionist	What's your new address then?
Jack	17 Rocksford Avenue, Chelmsford.
Receptionist	Is that R – O – C – K – S – F – O – R – D ?
Jack	Yes, that's right The postcode for Chelmsford is CM3 94Y.
Receptionist	Thanks. What time would you like to have your interview?
Jack	When are you open?
Receptionist	The office is open from 8 a.m. to 5 p.m. but we can schedule appointments from 8 in the morning through till 7 at night.
Jack	That's great – the evening would suit me better.
Receptionist	How about 6 on Thursday night?
Jack	Terrific. Do I come here for the interview?
Receptionist	Yes, but because the office closes at 5, the door will be locked. Just ring the doorbell and the counsellor will let you in.
Jack	Where's the doorbell?
Receptionist	It's just under the sign.

Jack arrives at the Counsellor's Office for his interview and meets one of the student counsellors.

As you listen to the rest of the conversation, answer Questions 6 – 10.

Before the conversation continues, read Questions 6 – 10.

SHORT PAUSE

Counsellor	Hi – you must be Jack. I'm Ellen Short – one of the student counsellors at Grisham College.
Jack	Nice to meet you Ellen.
Counsellor	I see you're an external student Jack. Do you find it difficult to do your assignments without going to lectures?
Jack	Oh, not really. We get really good study guides that have all the information we need but we can also contact the lecturers by phone or email. It's been a great course.
Counsellor	That's good to hear. Now what can I help you with?
Jack	I'd like to talk about my career options. I'm teaching French at the moment and studying linguistics but I've been offered a research position at the university. I really don't know whether to take the position or not.
Counsellor	Oh I see. Do you enjoy teaching?
Jack	Well, yes – for the most part I do. I find teaching very satisfying – it's great to see students do well. And of course, I love the summer holiday – six weeks at the end of the school-year is fantastic.
Counsellor	Yes, but you'd get a long summer holiday at the university wouldn't you?
Jack	Yes – I think it's an even longer period.
Counsellor	Is there anything that you don't like about teaching?
Jack	Oh yes – lazy students who don't want to do any work or the ones that behave badly and disturb the rest of the class. That can be very difficult. I guess I am a little tired of teaching. The pay for teachers isn't very good either. In fact, I find it difficult to save any money from my salary.
Counsellor	I see. So, what do you think the advantages of working at the university will be?
Jack	Well, as I said, it's a research position which means I wouldn't be teaching – it would be nice to have a break. The pay will be much better than what I'm getting at the moment and of course, I'd still get a long summer holiday. And, professionally I think working at a university would help me in the future.
Counsellor	So are there any negatives?
Jack	Well, the only real negative that I can think of is that I'll be working by myself. I'm not really used to that. It seems with teaching that there's always somebody around – whether it's the students or teachers or parents.
Counsellor	So, you can only think of one disadvantage?
Jack	Well, I'd have to travel a longer distance. At the moment, I just walk to school but I'd have to drive for about 35 minutes to the university.
Counsellor	Right Jack – let's write down all of the advantages and disadvantages in both jobs.
Jack	Yes - that sounds like a good idea.
Counsellor	Right – let's start with the advantages of teaching...

That is the end of Section 1. You now have ½ minute to check your answers.

Now turn to Section 2 of your Listening Question Booklet.

SECTION 2

You will hear Constable Andrew Gray talking about a problem in the Darlinghurst area to a group of international students at The University of Technology International Centre.

As you listen to the talk answer Questions 11 to 15.

Before you listen, look at Questions 11 to 15.

[SHORT PAUSE]

CONSTABLE GRAY:

Before I start, I'd like to thank the University of Technology International Centre for allowing me to come and talk to you all this afternoon. The reason for my visit is to outline a problem that female international visitors and students have been having in the Darlinghurst area.

For the last month or so, thieves have been targeting the area snatching handbags and backpacks from unsuspecting women. As you probably know, Darlinghurst is very popular with tourists for shopping and sightseeing and it's also a popular meeting place for students. There are lots of cafes and coffee shops and unfortunately, we've had some thieves taking advantage of these conditions. The thieves are young and fit – they grab the bag from the woman's shoulder or out of her hand when she's involved with something else – you know, deep in conversation or window-shopping - so they grab the bag and then run away very quickly. By the time the victim realizes what's happened, the young man's out of sight and there's little hope of catching him. The victims are always female and almost always, a visitor to the area. When these incidents first started, the victims were always by themselves but now it seems they're becoming braver and targeting women in groups. Age doesn't seem to matter to the thieves – it's just a matter of opportunity. They look for someone who isn't consciously protecting their bag and for a place with an easy getaway – you know, not too crowded.

We've only had two of these bag-snatchers almost caught when the victims chased after them. Unfortunately, on both occasions, as soon as the women reached the thief, he threw the bag right at them and then escaped. One woman was hurt quite badly. They really are brazen.

We don't encourage you to chase these thieves – there are many small laneways and streets in Darlinghurst that the thieves can escape into. We just don't know what they're likely to do and we certainly don't want anyone to get hurt.

So, what can you do? Well, unfortunately, not much but we are asking that you be aware of this danger. If possible, walk with a friend while you're in the area – hang onto your bags carefully – don't leave your bags on the ground at one of the many cafés while you have a coffee or a meal and don't leave it on a chair or tabletop – in other words, be alert at all times and conscious of your bag while you're in the area.

We'd also caution you about carrying anything too valuable in your bags. Don't for instance, carry too much cash and please ensure that you know the details of all of your credit cards. It seems like the thieves are not only after cash. They've been using credit cards illegally on the Internet to purchase goods or access pornographic sites. So some of our targets not only lose the cash they have in their bags but they get a nasty surprise when their credit card bills arrive at the end of the month. It's vital that you keep your credit card details and report your loss to police.

Before the final part of the talk, look at Questions 16 to 20.

[SHORT PAUSE]

Now you will hear the rest of the talk. Answer Questions 16 to 20.

If you take these precautions and still get robbed, please contact your nearest police station. You can of course come to the Darlinghurst Police Station but this isn't necessary. The police will need to get certain details – in particular your name, your contact phone number and the time that the robbery took place. We'll also ask you for the exact location of the incident. Please take note of the nearest cross-street or laneway. A lot of the victims haven't been able to tell us this, but it is vital if we're going to catch these thieves – or try to remember the name of the nearest shop. We are trying to establish any patterns to the thefts. We will also need a full description of the bag or article that was snatched. Most of the bags are found discarded nearby with the cash and credit cards gone. Obviously you'll need to cancel your credit cards as a matter of urgency. The only protection you have against being made responsible for illegal use of your credit card, is if you report the card stolen before the thieves can use it.

We are confident that these thieves will stop their practice if we show that we're aware of their presence and limit their profits. The Darlinghurst police have some plain-clothes, female detectives in the area now and we're sure to catch them. Getting accurate locations of these incidents is vital.

It's not our intention to frighten any of you but we do want you to be aware of the problem and hopefully avoid any trouble.

Are there any questions?

That is the end of Section 2. You now have ½ minute to check your answers.

Now turn to Section 3 of your Listening Question Booklet.

SECTION 3

In this section you will hear two students talking to their tutor about a presentation they are going to give.

First, look at Questions 21 to 30.

[SHORT PAUSE]

Now listen to the discussion and answer Questions 21 to 30.

Tutor	Jane and Rick – nice to see you both. How's your presentation coming along?
Jane	Well, that's why we're here- we'd like to ask you for some clarification.
Rick	Yes, I'm afraid we are not quite sure that we understand exactly what you'd like us to include in our report.
Tutor	I'm glad that you came to see me – but the deadline is only three weeks away – are you going to have it done by then?
Jane	Oh yes – we think we've done most of the time-consuming work – we just have to pull the information from the survey together and present it in the right format.
Tutor	That's good to hear – collating is the fun part. Did you follow the steps I outlined in the questionnaire survey?
Jane	Yes. We found that the most difficult step was the first one – defining our objectives and then of course writing the items to match.
Tutor	What topic did you choose?
Rick	We decided to survey international students about their experiences and the challenges that they faced when they first came to Australia.
Tutor	Right – that's a very broad topic to survey…
Jane	We found that out the hard way.
Rick	Sure did – but we are happy with our work, aren't we Jane?
Jane	Yes, so far.
Rick	Yes, so far. We handed out almost 400 surveys to international students – not all from Longholm either. We sent 150 to the Western Australian Education Department in Perth and 120 to Griffin Technical College in Melbourne.
Tutor	I'm pleased to hear that you didn't restrict the survey to Longholm.
Rick	No, we wanted to find out the responses from a range of international students in Australia, as opposed to the experiences at one tertiary institution only.
Jane	We chose a technical college as well as a university campus and a high school – that gave us access to students of different ages and different disciplines.
Tutor	So how many respondents did you get?
Jane	Well, in our trial of the survey, we received 44 out of the 50 surveys – over 88% – but that was tightly controlled. We didn't expect such a high percentage of returns from the actual survey itself. We had hoped to receive about 70%.
Rick	We were both a bit surprised really – we got over 320 surveys returned – 322 to be exact. That's 80%!
Tutor	322 out of 400 – yes that is an impressive rate of response. Did you have to do a lot of follow-up work to get those?
Rick	We sent out some postcard reminders to some students who hadn't returned the surveys by the deadline and from them we received another 38 surveys back.
Jane	Rick had written a very persuasive transmittal letter that accompanied the survey. In the letter, he appealed to their individual contributions so that the situations for international students might improve.

Tutor	Transmittal letters can be very effective – well done! So it sounds like you've followed the correct procedure up until now – you set your objectives and wrote items to match those objectives. You gave out trial surveys – collected them – chased the late surveys. I hope you had also analysed your pre-test trial results before sending out the actual surveys.
Jane	Yes, analysing the data from the trial survey was very useful. We checked all of the responses to each item in the pre-test and found a pattern in some items that had been left unanswered. We re-wrote those items that were ambiguous or open to different interpretation. The actual survey worked better because of this.
Tutor	Trial surveys can be invaluable. So you sent out your transmittal letters with the survey and got a high percentage of responses. You shouldn't have any problems making conclusions for your survey.
Rick	Yes, we have collated all of our data – which took ages after we received the actual surveys back. We haven't started to make conclusions yet because we are not sure how to begin our report.
Tutor	You've done the majority of the work – as Jane said, the time-consuming part. It'll probably help you to know the three main criteria I'll be using to mark your presentations. The first is the quality of your questions' objectives – make sure that you don't give me aims of the survey. I want clear objectives for each item. The second criterion is the quality of the items in your questionnaire.
Rick	We are quite confident with the items. We analysed the pre-test trial quite thoroughly.
Tutor	Yes, you have already completed that section obviously. The third criterion will be judging the quality of your analysis of the data and the conclusions that you draw. This is always the most interesting part of the presentations for me.
Rick	Should this include percentages and tables and graphs to display the data?
Tutor	Absolutely – make your conclusions as visual as possible. They should be easy to read and easy to follow. Ensure that the tables and graphs are clearly labelled with appropriate headings and only include relevant data.
Rick	That's great – thank you very much. We know what we need to do next.
Jane	Yes – thanks a lot.
Tutor	My pleasure – I look forward to seeing your presentation in March.

That is the end of Section 3. You now have ½ minute to check your answers.

Now turn to Section 4 of your Listening Question Booklet.

SECTION 4

You will hear a lecture about Project Management being given by a university lecturer.

First, look at Questions 31 to 40.

[SHORT PAUSE]

Now listen to the lecture and answer Questions 31 to 40.

LECTURER:

I'd like to begin today with a quick review of last week's lecture. We saw the definition of project management as something which has a clear beginning and a clear completion date with goals, a budget and a schedule. We saw its presence in the private and public sectors in many different industries. You'll also remember that we outlined the life cycle as it were, of a project and looked at the first of a four-stage cycle – establishing the limits of the project.

Today, we're going to talk broadly about the second stage of project management – developing a plan for the project. Next week we'll focus on the implementation of the project and then, the final stage - its evaluation.

Let's get started on today's topic, though – planning the project. The success of a project will depend on the skills and care which you put in at this initial planning stage. Planning is not only necessary in terms of budget or cost, it's also crucial that you consider the time-frame of a project and the standards which you'll be expected to provide. These three elements are of course, integrated. Project-planning is best conducted as a team – you might have to take responsibility for handing over the final plan but without a team behind you, you'll find it almost impossible to plan effectively.

We'll discuss budgetary planning firstly because that is, of course, what you are most likely to be evaluated on by your own manager. Before drawing up a budget, you'll need to understand the time-frame involved to carry out the work and the standard of delivery at which the labour and materials are to be supplied. Now, this is arguably the most difficult to plan for. You'll never plan completely accurately for a project in terms of money but you will become better at planning <u>realistically</u>. And it is this part of the planning process that you will do last.

The best way to plan the cost of a project is to consider all the factors involved and how those factors relate to time and standard of delivery. Write these down on a spreadsheet format and begin the task of costing and estimating. The company that you're employed by will always have their own systems in place for doing this. They will also indicate the kind of profit they are looking for – usually in percentage terms.

The second stage of planning is the allocation of time to a project and for this, you'll have to canvass others for help. Only by asking the advice and opinions of those with expertise in the field, will you be able to establish the size of each unit of work to be completed and the order in which those units of work should be carried out. Remember that some units of work may be done simultaneously but many cannot. In your tutorials this week, you'll be introduced to the Gant Chart – that's G-A-N-T. This method of planning project activities has been very successful in the field of project management. The complete set of tasks involved in a project are identified and then planned in relation to each other. You'll soon discover that organizing and prioritizing activities is quite an art-form.

The third part of your planning as I said, will affect your money and time considerations and that is the standard of delivery that the project demands. These standards will be outlined in the tender documents if they've been your guide or the masterplan from which you're working. Always make sure that you've got ALL of the project-related documents that are available. For every unit of work that is to be completed, you'll have to write specifications – they are detailed descriptions outlining specific standards of quality in materials and labour. If these specifications are not carefully written and then complied with, the project is unlikely to be successful. These specifications will be referred to many times once the project is underway.

You will also have to deal with a Quality Assurance Manager at this stage who will advise you on the standards which need to be met. Quality management has become a valued component in successful project management companies.

I've provided you with an outline of the planning process for project management but you'll be looking at these three elements in more depth in your tutorials this week.

That is the end of Section 4 and the end of the Listening Test. You now have ½ minute to check your answers.

[PAUSE]

You now have 10 minutes to transfer your answers to your Answer Booklet.

TEST 3

SECTION 1

You will hear two friends talking outside an examination room about working over the vacation period. First, look at Questions 1 to 5.

[SHORT PAUSE]

You will see that there is an example already done for you. For this question only the conversation relating to the example will be played first.

Crystal	Hi Peter – I'm so pleased that exam's over!
Peter	Me too Crystal – I'm exhausted. I stayed up late studying last night and then got up early this morning.
Crystal	Well, you can rest now – we're on holidays for three glorious weeks.

Peter said he stayed up late studying last night, so C is the correct answer.

Now we shall begin. You should answer the questions as you listen because you will not hear the recording a second time.

Now listen carefully and answer Questions 1 to 5.

Crystal	Hi Peter – I'm so pleased that exam's over!
Peter	Me too, Crystal – I'm exhausted. I stayed up late last night studying and then got up early this morning.
Crystal	Well, you can rest now – we're on holidays for three glorious weeks.
Peter	That is a nice thought. Unfortunately though, I'm broke and if I'm going to have enough money to get through next semester, I'll have to get a job over the holidays.
Crystal	Yes, I've been thinking the same thing myself. As much as I'd like to go home to see my family, I think I'll have to get a job as well. Have you got any ideas or contacts?
Peter	Well, as a matter of fact, I'm going to go to the Student Employment Office. Do you want to come with me?
Crystal	Sure, if you don't mind. Where is it?
Peter	Let me see – (*TAKES OUT PAPER*) – I've got a map here of the campus. It's up here in Y Block.
Crystal	Oh boy – we're a long way away from there! We've just come out of N Block – here we are here.
Peter	Yes, N Block. Well, we can turn right and follow Circular Drive around but that's the long way. What's the building opposite us?
Crystal	That's the International Centre – I learnt English there before starting my Bachelor of Business.
Peter	Oh right – I see, it says I Block. I guess I stands for International. Well, let's cross Circular Drive and walk up to the right -
Crystal	No, there's lots of trees and gardens there – we'd better go to the left of the building. You can't get through otherwise.
Peter	OK – we'll head past D Block, go between B and C Blocks and then across the sports fields to Y Block.
Crystal	OK, but I'm really hungry. How about going to the student canteen before we get to Y Block? It's just on the other side of A Block – near the main entrance.
Peter	Good idea – I didn't have breakfast this morning. I'm starving! Let's go.

Peter and Crystal arrive at the Student Employment Office and the receptionist meets them.

As you listen to the rest of the conversation, answer Questions 6 to 10.

Before the conversation continues, read Questions 6 to 10.

[SHORT PAUSE]

Receptionist	Good morning – can I help you?
Peter	Good morning – yes, we'd both like to find some vacation work.
Receptionist	Right – for this vacation period?
Peter & Crystal	Yes. Mm – hmm.
Receptionist	Have you registered with us?
Peter & Crystal:	No.
Receptionist	Oh – you have left it a bit late. Students usually register with us around mid-semester.
Peter	Really?
Receptionist	Yes, but never mind. You will need to register, but before you do that, you'll need to be interviewed by one of our consultants.
Peter	Oh – I thought you would just give us a list of job vacancies and we would contact those places directly.
Receptionist	No, we don't give out contacts until after you've been interviewed and registered.
Peter	I see.
Receptionist	Would you like to make an appointment to have an interview?
Peter & Crystal	Yes, please. Yes – as soon as possible.
Receptionist	Let me see – today's Thursday 11th. Our consultants are here tomorrow but they are going on a Staff In-service from next Monday to Wednesday. So, it's either Friday – that's tomorrow or next Thursday.
Peter	Couldn't we see one of them this afternoon?
Receptionist	No, they are fully booked I'm afraid. End of semester is the busiest time for job placements, as you can imagine. There has been a cancellation for tomorrow morning at 9:30 or you can come after 2 tomorrow afternoon.
Peter	Can we be interviewed together?
Receptionist	Yes, I'm sure that would be OK.
Peter	Crystal, is 9:30 all right with you?
Crystal	Yes that suits me. Actually, I'm going to the dentist tomorrow – let me check the time. (LOOKS UP DIARY) Hang on, the dentist is at 9, so could we make it at 2?
Peter	No problem.
Receptionist	OK – that's for 2 o'clock then. What's your surname?
Peter	Pastel. P – A – S – T – E – L. Peter's my first name.
Receptionist	Thanks – and yours?
Crystal	My surname's Lu. L – U. My first name's Crystal – that's C – R – Y – S – T – A – L.
Receptionist	Right – a contact phone number please?
Peter	My mobile is 0412 987 35.
Receptionist	Thank you and I'll need your Student Number as well, so I can access your files.
Peter	Mine is B (for Business) 7 2 3 4 double 6.
Crystal	And mine is B (for Business as well) I 6 9 double zero, double 1.
Receptionist	That's BI69 double 0, double 1 for you Peter and...
Crystal & Peter	No, that's mine – Wrong way around.
	(ALL LAUGH)
Receptionist	Oops! – it's BI69 double zero, double 1 for Crystal, and B7234 double 6 for Peter. I'll just put an arrow next to your names to show what I've done wrong! Right then – see you both.
Peter & Crystal	Bye. Thanks a lot.

That is the end of Section 1. You now have ½ minute to check your answers.

[PAUSE]

Now turn to Section 2 of your Listening Question Booklet.

SECTION 2

You will hear a speaker from the Brisbane Festival talking to some international visitors in Brisbane, Australia.

As you listen to the talk, answer Questions 11 to 20.

Before you listen, look at Questions 11 to 20.

[SHORT PAUSE]

SPEAKER:

Good evening – umm, I've been asked to tell you all about the Brisbane Festival which is being held here in Brisbane from September 8th to October 6th. You are all of course, welcome to come along to the various activities that we have planned while you're visiting our city. We're happy to announce that we have some free tickets which I'll hand out later.

The Brisbane Festival is held every year in a number of venues around Brisbane, not only to show off our own local talent but also to celebrate the incredible talent that we have in the Australian and the South-East Asian region. It's a great time for us to catch up with our interstate and international friends and we're thrilled that this year we have a record number of performances from South-East Asian participants. We have seen an increased amount of interest from European and American artists in recent years and we welcome them as well.

Our goal is to bring people together through art by making art accessible to everyone. The Brisbane Festival aims to promote cultural understanding and interaction.

Right. Well – as you experienced today, we have a wonderful climate here in Brisbane – our average temperature is about 24° Celsius and we have something like 290 sunny days a year. Naturally we want to take advantage of this – so we've scheduled performances in public places such as Southbank Parklands and the City Gardens as well as the more traditional indoor venues – the Performing Arts Centre, Brisbane Convention Centre, the Brisbane Power House and some of our university campuses.

I'll hand out a copy of the program shortly but I'd like to tell you about some of the highlights of the program and encourage you to enjoy as many of them as possible. I can also give you details on how to get to the venues.

The first event that I'll be seeing is the Israel Philharmonic Orchestra at the Performing Arts Centre tomorrow night – that's September 8. It starts at 8 p.m. and because there is one performance only, you should get there well before 8 p.m. – say 7:30 at the latest. And then for something completely different, MONKEY which is a play - is showing at the Powerhouse at 6:30 on the following night. So you will have two late nights in a row but they are such different performances that I think you have to see both of them. MONKEY is based on a 16th Century Chinese story – you might have seen the television series… I can't wait for that one.

We also have plenty of music on the itinerary - for those of you who like to hear arias, world-renowned soprano Sumi Jo is performing with the Queensland Orchestra on September 11th. She will be starting at 8 p.m. – if you can't make it then, though, she will be performing some opera at later performances. And talking about music, Festival Club is going to be held every evening from Wednesdays to Saturdays at the City Gardens – Festival Club features music from around the world. I'm sure this will be very popular with the younger members of our group and you'll feel very relaxed in the cool, spring Brisbane evenings under the stars … The City Gardens is one of our most popular venues.

For those of you who are interested in Visual Arts, from September 13 – no, I'm sorry September 14 – the Art Gallery will be displaying works in the Asia-Pacific Triennial. There are details of that display in the handout.

If you like drama, you'll have to see Slava's Snowshow the next day, at the Performing Arts Centre. It is a Russian production which has been wowing audiences from Moscow to London. It starts at 6 –

again, don't be late because I'm sure that will be very popular and the Performing Arts Centre has limited seating.

Barbara Fordham will be performing a series of concerts at the City Football Club from September 20 – she has the most wonderful voice and you won't want to miss one of her concerts particularly if you like blues music. Concerts start at 8 – as I said at the City Football Club.

We also have a Poetry and Writers Festival happening in Brisbane if you're into that. The Poetry Festival starts on September 22th and the Writers Festival will be on from October 4 to October 6.

And if you don't go to anything else, you simply must go to the Opera Under the Stars at City Gardens. This will be the grand finale on October 6th – it really will be fantastic and I expect there will be fireworks and all sorts of exciting things going on. So remember that one, Opera Under the Stars – starting at 6 on October 6.

OK – that's it from me. I really hope that you take the time to join in whenever you can with the Brisbane Festival celebrations. If you want any more information please come and see me - the information booklets and tickets are at the front door. Have a good night everyone and enjoy your time in Brisbane.

That is the end of Section 2. You now have ½ minute to check your answers.

Now turn to Section 3 of your Listening Question Booklet.

SECTION 3

In this section you will hear two students presenting a tutorial on two Asian countries, Singapore and Malaysia.

First, look at Questions 21 to 30.

[SHORT PAUSE]

Now listen to the two students and answer Questions 21 to 30.

Tutor	Nancy and Jenny are presenting the first of our profiles on Asia today. You looked at Singapore and Malaysia didn't you?
Nancy	Yes, and we found lots of similarities between the two countries.
Tutor	Did you follow the outline that I gave you?
Jenny	Yes we did. Um, first of all the total land area of Singapore is 630 square kilometres, whilst Malaysia's was 329,758 square kilometres. Obviously Malaysia is a much larger nation with a bigger population – almost 24 million. It is bigger than Australia's population, in fact – we have 19,700,000. Um, Singapore has just over 3 million.
Tutor	Did you look at their population mix?
Nancy	The population of both Malaysia and Singapore are multi-racial – they each have a mixture of Malays, Chinese, Indians and other ethnic groups as well, who all live quite harmoniously together. The breakdown of the population is different though. In Malaysia, the Malays or Bumiputeras as they are called, outnumber the Chinese and the Indians. They make up about 65% of the population. In Singapore, three quarters of the population is Chinese with only a few hundred thousand Malays and Indians. English is widely used in Malaysia as well as in Singapore.
Jenny	Yes, they all study compulsory English at school and adults use English a lot in their daily lives. For many years, Singaporeans have been sending their children abroad to study in English-speaking countries. And in recent years, Malaysians are also studying overseas and getting overseas work experience.
Tutor	Australia has had a fairly stable relationship with Singapore over the years – can you briefly talk about that?
Nancy	Umm, yes. Singapore and Australia have always maintained a friendly and warm relationship. As Jen said, many students come to Australia to study here and often they stay here to work. Similarly, lots of Australians live and work in Singapore. Singapore

was one of the first Asian countries to really take advantage of its geographical location and the technological advances that were made at the end of last century. It has a strong economy.

Jenny	Singapore and Australia signed an expanded trade accord in February which covers all sorts of subjects from education through to customs procedures at the airports! It's accepted that this accord will really strengthen ties between the two countries.
Nancy	So, trade between Singapore and Australia is continuing to grow but we're not one of Singapore's top three trading partners. They're the US, Japan and Malaysia.
Jenny	Yes, and interestingly but not surprisingly I guess, Malaysia's top three trading partners are the US, Japan and Singapore.
Tutor	Yes, Singapore and Malaysia are neighbours so you would expect that. What did you discover about the relationship between Malaysia and Australia?
Jenny	Well, um, it hasn't been as stable as Singapore and Australia's friendship. Malaysians and Australians get along well on a personal level – there have been an increasing number of tourists travelling between the two countries. So, it isn't just the students who are coming here. Historically, Australia and Malaysia and for that matter Singapore as well, have a lot in common – you know, with the British Colonialists. Malaysia, now, doesn't want to blindly follow western ideas, which is fair enough.
Tutor	Yes – this is something that we'll talk about later in the semester – Australia's international relations in the region.
Jenny	There do seem to be misunderstandings and disagreements between Malaysia and Australia, but diplomats say that these are exaggerated by the media.
Tutor	Yes, we all know the power that the media has. Was there anything else?
Nancy	Well, um, yes – what I found was that Singaporeans are generally regarded as well-educated, well-travelled - knowledgeable. They enjoy a quality of life that is envied in other countries – especially in other Asian countries. The Singaporean government is spending a lot of money on education and technology.
Tutor	Is this going to continue – did you look at the government's agenda for the future?
Nancy	They are developing a knowledge-based economy. Unlike other South-East Asian countries, Singapore hasn't been dependent on the production and export of commodities. They intend to be IT driven with a highly skilled economy.
Tutor	I see and how did this differ in Malaysia?
Jenny	Well, the Malaysians are very enterprising people. They're well-educated and highly skilled too. Like the Singaporeans, they've got a strong work ethic. We both felt that of the two countries, Malaysians were much more Asian in their way of thinking, although they seem to mix Eastern and Western traditions easily. This could be one of the reasons that tourism is doing so well in Malaysia. The economy once relied almost solely on the export of raw materials, but that's changed a lot. All the experts say that Malaysia has a huge future.
Tutor	You have obviously enjoyed your research. I'm sure you'll enjoy learning more about the region as we continue on with the other overviews.

That is the end of Section 3. You now have ½ minute to check your answers.

Now turn to Section 4 of your Listening Question Booklet.

SECTION 4

You will hear an introductory lecture about vegetarianism being given by a nutritionist.

First, look at Questions 31 to 40.

[SHORT PAUSE]

Now listen to the lecture and answer Questions 31 to 40.

LECTURER:

You will all have a vague understanding of what being a vegetarian is all about. Vegetarianism has been practised for thousands of years. The simplest definition is someone who doesn't eat meat of course - but does abstaining from eating meat include seafood and chicken? The fact of the matter is that people adopt the label "vegetarian" but still eat meat, at least to varying degrees. Within true vegetarianism, that is where a vegetarian is someone who doesn't eat any meat at all, there are three sub-groups. A lacto-ovo-vegetarian eats no meat but does consume dairy products and eggs. The second sub-group, lacto-vegetarians, also don't eat meat but while they will consume dairy products, they don't eat eggs. And then of course there are vegans – people with a strict vegetarian diet that don't eat any animal product or by-product including honey. In fact, they don't even wear woollen, leather or silk garments. So just keep in mind that there is an obvious sliding scale here when people talk about vegetarianism – there are those that perhaps like to think of themselves as vegetarian just because they don't eat red meat right through to those strict vegans who will only eat vegetables, fruit, beans or pulses – that is, food that has been grown.

For our purposes today, we'll be talking about vegetarians as those people who don't eat any form of meat at all – red meat, fish or poultry – but do use dairy products and eggs. Lacto-vegetarians and vegans are not the majority anyway.

With that definition in mind, let's review the myriad of reasons given for adopting a vegetarian diet. These include all sorts of preposterous theories that claim all humans should be vegetarian simply because it's natural or that humans are naturally vegetarian because biologically we resemble plant-eaters! In the real world, vegetarians generally speaking, accept that humans are omnivores – they are capable of eating both plant and meat foods. Statistics show that the majority of vegetarians have adopted a vegetarian diet because of their religious beliefs as in the case of Hindus and Buddhists for example, or because of health-related concerns – that is, they see vegetarianism as a healthier alternative.

Look - that's not to say there aren't other reasons – some people just don't like the taste of meat and others simply can't afford to buy it. A significant number of vegetarians are animal liberationists who are against the killing of animals for human consumption. These vegetarians have taken the step of refusing to eat meat and in doing so, show that they don't condone those killings. They see the whole industry as barbaric. In the past, at least in my social circle, such a cause was seen as noble and many of us held vegetarians in high regard - they lived up to their beliefs. In more recent times, as we see the disastrous impact of introduced hooved animals on lands and the amount of resources used to feed stock at the expense of using arable land for crops, their noble cause has been ecologically justified as well. Land resources and arable lands in particular, are scarce and becoming scarcer. Perhaps it is wrong to allocate these resources to raising those animals which provide us with a food source that we can live without.

But is this the case? Can we live without meat in our diet and is living a vegetarian lifestyle indeed more healthy as advocates would have us believe? Vegetarians claim that a well-balanced vegetarian diet will supply all the essential nutrients we need to be healthy. In Western societies, as late as 20 or 30 years ago, there were many myths about vegetarianism. Those switching to vegetarianism would be warned about serious vitamin deficiencies.

Statistically, though, the vegetarians are supported in their claim that vegetarians are healthier than meat-eaters. The incidence of heart disease and cancer for example, are significantly lower in non-meat-eaters. In fact it's claimed that the risks from certain cancers are reduced by up to 40% in a vegetarian diet. And let's face it, in modern Western society with our concerns regarding obesity, you don't see too many overweight vegetarians do you? Vegetarians consume less fat and protein than we do and the fat that they do consume is in the main, unsaturated – which is what has been recently labelled "good fat". On the other hand, animal fats tend to be saturated and an increased intake of saturated fats can lead to high cholesterol. Respiratory problems too, seem less common in vegetarians but this is also the case with meat-eaters who include a lot of fruit and vegetables in their diet. The UK Vegetarian Society's website quotes medical research has shown that on average, a lifelong vegetarian visits hospital 22% less than a meat-eater.

The fact that the number of practising vegetarians has almost doubled in the last fifteen years, speaks volumes about the way our concerns for healthy living have changed. The reasons given for this increase has been according to a recent survey, 94% due to the perceived health benefits associated with a vegetarian lifestyle. Doctors and nutritionists and responsible groups like the Vegetarian Society are rightly concerned that those adopting the vegetarian diet do so in an informed way. There are health benefits to be gained by turning vegetarian, but there are also guidelines that need to be followed – Vitamin B12 for instance and recommended amounts of iron are not easily found in a vegetarian diet, and yet they are vital for healthy living.

So, where can such vitamin and mineral replacements be found in the vegetarian diet? Well, for the average vegetarian, good sources of iron are spinach, prune juice or dried fruit. Vegetarians are advised to eat these foods with fruit juices which will increase the amount of iron absorbed. B12 on the other hand, is not as readily available because it is only found to all intents and purposes in meat, fish and dairy products. This vitamin is one which vegetarians find difficult to replace. However, as I said, low amounts of B12 can be found in dairy products as well as soy products or seaweed. For the stricter lacto-vegetarian and vegan, B12 can be obtained from foods that have been fortified with the vitamin. Vegetable margarines, some soy products and breakfast cereals are the most common sources.

The key to a healthy vegetarian diet is the same as any other diet – eat a wide variety of foods including grains, fruit and vegetables, beans, pulses and nuts. Vitamins and minerals must be included in the vegetarian diet, just as they have to be included in a non-vegetarian diet. You can argue all you like about vegetarians being healthier, but I'd suggest that you consider a well-balanced diet first and foremost. Whether or not you include meat is up to you. A good vegetarian diet closely matches the dietary recommendations for a healthy meat-eating diet. There's an excellent website which I suggest you look at if you want further information on vegetarianism – it's www.vegsoc.org.

That is the end of Section 4 and the end of the Listening Test.

You now have ½ minute to check your answers.

[PAUSE]

You now have 10 minutes to transfer your answers to your Answer Booklet.

TEST 4

SECTION 1

You are going to listen to two university students talking about libraries in Australia. First, look at Questions 1 to 4.

[SHORT PAUSE]

You will see that there is an example already done for you. For this question only, the conversation relating to the example will be played first.

Mary Ann	What's wrong Yumi – you look very serious.
Yumi	Oh. Hi Mary Ann. I've just been given the assessment guide for Law – my major – and there are lots of assignments.
Mary Ann	You'll be spending a lot of time in the library then.
Yumi	That's my problem – I don't know anything about libraries in Australia.
Mary Ann	Well, don't worry about that Yumi. Librarians here are really friendly and most of them are extremely helpful.

Yumi said she doesn't know anything about libraries in Australia. So B is the correct answer.

Now we shall begin. You should answer the questions as you listen because you will not hear the recording a second time.

Now listen carefully and answer Questions 1 to 4.

Mary Ann	What's wrong Yumi – you look very serious.
Yumi	Oh. Hi Mary Ann. I've just been given the assessment guide for Law – my major – and there are lots of assignments.
Mary Ann	You'll be spending a lot of time in the library then.
Yumi	That's my problem – I don't know anything about libraries in Australia.
Mary Ann	Well, don't worry about that Yumi. Librarians here are really friendly and most of them are extremely helpful.
Yumi	That's good to hear. My flatmate said I should join the local library – do you think that I need to?
Mary Ann	Well, I think it'd be a good idea. They probably won't have many Law books in the library but you'll be surprised at what they do have. Australian libraries are generally very well-resourced and hey, if nothing else, you can get free Internet access.
Yumi	Is it easy for international students to join?
Mary Ann	Yes, Li Yun has just joined. All you need is your Student Card (or some other I.D.) and an account or bill that has your Australian address on it.
Yumi	Like a phone bill or an electricity bill – would that be OK?
Mary Ann	Yeah, that's all. It's very easy. They encourage people to join the library and you can borrow lots of books as well as video and audio tapes or CDs. The newspaper is available too if you've got time to stay at the library and read it!
Yumi	Will it cost much to join the library?
Mary Ann	Joining libraries here doesn't cost anything but you'll have to pay a fine if you return your books after the due date – it's about 10 cents per book per day.
Yumi	How long can I borrow books for?
Mary Ann	The loan period for books is about a month but you can easily extend the time for another month if you want to – you can even do it over the phone but it has to be arranged before the due date.
Yumi	What about the university library?
Mary Ann	Haven't you been there yet?
Yumi	No, not yet. I was sick for the Orientation Week and I missed out on the campus tour.
Mary Ann	Well, Yumi - I've got an hour before my next lecture. Why don't we walk up together and have a look around?
Yumi	Oh, that'd be great Mary Ann – I'd really appreciate it.

Yumi and Mary Ann arrive at the main entrance to the university library.

As you listen to the rest of the conversation, answer Questions 5 to 10.

Before the conversation continues, read Questions 5 to 10.

[SHORT PAUSE]

Mary Ann	This is the main entrance. Let's go in.
Yumi	It's very big isn't it?
Mary Ann	Yes, but here's a map which will help you. Can you see that it's a kind of L shape?
Yumi	Oh yes. Is that the Circulations Desk in front of us?
Mary Ann	Yes, that's where all of the incoming and outgoing loans are registered. When you return a book, just put it in the large box over there – see it's marked RETURNS – just to the right of the desk.
Yumi	Yes I see. Can I use the computers behind the desk to access the Internet?
Mary Ann	Those computers are for the library's database search system only. There are computers in the IT Block which we passed on our way here to the library. Anyway, you can search for a book by typing in the title, author, topic or a key word.
Yumi	Are the computers easy to use?
Mary Ann	Yes, very easy. Even I can use them!
Yumi	Does it give a catalogue number after you do the search?
Mary Ann	Yes it does. It'll also tell you in which section of the library to find the book. The library is divided into three sections – straight ahead, behind the Circulations Desk is the Monograph Collection – that just means you can borrow these materials for normal loans.
Yumi	Monograph Collection? Yes, I see.
Mary Ann	The section behind the photocopiers is for all of the Serial Publications – that means journals and magazines and newspapers of course.
Yumi	Mm hmm.
Mary Ann	And the most important section for us is the Reference Section – you'll use it a lot! Unfortunately, the books in this section can't be borrowed – you have to use them in the library. It's over there, past the quiet study area.
Yumi	I see. So do I need to join or register here, or do I have automatic borrowing rights as a student?
Mary Ann	As long as you have your student card, you can borrow books from the Monograph Collection. Anyone else can access the rest of the library.
Yumi	What if I can't find a particular book?
Mary Ann	That's what the staff are there for Yumi. Just go to the Advisors' Desk, take a request card and fill in the details of what you are looking for.
Yumi	Where's the Advisors' Desk?
Mary Ann	It's just over there – the desk at the entrance to the Quiet Study Area.
Yumi	Right – well, I think I'll have a look now to see if I can find any of the Recommended Texts for my first Law Assignment.
Mary Ann	Yes, good idea. Texts on the recommended lists from the lecturers are very popular and you should try to borrow them from the library as soon as you get your list.

That is the end of Section 1. You now have ½ minute to check your answers.

Now turn to Section 2 of your Listening Question Booklet.

SECTION 2

You will hear Inspector Jack Dunne talking about International Drivers' Licenses at an information session for international travellers.

As you listen to the first part of the talk answer Questions 11 to 16.

Before you listen, look at Questions 11 to 16.

[SHORT PAUSE]

JACK DUNNE:

I'm sure that you have all heard about International Driving Licenses. They've been around since 1949, when the United Nations gave approval for their use. This meant that travellers could drive freely in the 186 countries that recognise the International Driving License system – regardless of the language that the drivers spoke. The only conditions were that the driver had to already hold a driving license in their home country and they had to be at least 18 years of age.

International Driver's Licenses are well-recognised – after all, they've been in use for over 50 years! To break the language barrier, the license is printed in 11 different languages but the last page of the booklet is always in French. As I said, it is a booklet – about the size of a passport – um, 10.8 by 15.25 centimetres to be exact. So it is easy to carry with your travel documents. It's not too thick or heavy either. Only seventeen pages. All of the pages are coloured white but the cover of the license is grey. It is a useful form of identification when you travel because it includes a passport-sized photograph and the driver's signature.

The International Driver's License can only be purchased from authorized travel associations in different countries but it can also be ordered on the Internet.

The cost of course varies from country to country and for the term or the duration of the license – for example, a one year license might cost approximately $40 whereas a three year license costs double that. A five year license will set you back about $100.

Before the final part of the talk, look at Questions 17 to 20.

[SHORT PAUSE]

Now you will hear the rest of the talk. Answer Questions 17 to 20.

Before I outline the four most important points to consider before rushing off to get your International Driver's License, I should probably mention that, yes, the International Driver's License covers all types of vehicles from motorbikes to trucks – but just as in your own country, you have to be qualified to drive such vehicles. You might like the idea of driving around the Australian outback on a motorbike or checking out the English countryside in a bus with all your mates, but you'll have to take the appropriate test before you set off!

OK – now the four main points: firstly, you cannot use an International License in the country in which it is issued – it is for international travel only. Some international students avoid this rule by ordering their licenses on the Internet which will ask them to nominate a "country of your choice" for that very purpose.

Secondly, some countries won't allow you to use an International License indefinitely. In Australia for example, you can only use the International License for a year – after that you must get an Australian Driving License. Other countries aren't as strict as that.

Drivers on International Licenses must abide by the road rules in the country that they are visiting. If you are caught breaking those road rules, you will have to pay the penalty – usually a fine. And if you are the cause of an accident, expect to pay for any damages that you are responsible for. Holding an International Driver's License does not give you the right to be reckless.

And yes, if you have been suspended or banned from driving in your own country, the same rules apply with an International Driver's License – you must have an existing Driver's License to apply for an International Driver's License. Some police will in fact, want to see both your International License and your own Driver's License – so carry both licenses with you to save wasting valuable time.

Finally, you don't have to take another driving test to get an International Driver's License – your own Driver's License is proof that you know how to drive. However, it is your responsibility to learn the road rules of the country that you are visiting and to understand what the different road signs mean. Police are not always understanding to foreign drivers! If you break road rules either deliberately or out of ignorance, expect to pay the price. Police are ultimately the same everywhere.

That is the end of Section 2. You now have ½ minute to check your answers.

Now turn to Section 3 of your Listening Question Booklet.

SECTION 3

In this section you will hear two students discussing the idea of joining a learning circle.

First, look at Questions 21 to 30.

[SHORT PAUSE]

Now listen to the discussion and answer Questions 21 to 30.

Anita	What's the reason for the learning circle you've set up Hamish?
Hamish	Well, it wasn't my idea - the Economics tutor suggested it actually – he said that it's a good way to make sure you put in the time needed for a particular subject. But for me, well, I thought that studying in a group like that would give me some incentive to study – I really need a reason to learn, you know, motivation, especially in economics!
Anita	Hmm, I guess study groups can give you discipline <u>and</u> motivation. They're both useful but my biggest problem is that I'm finding economics quite difficult. I think I need extra help just to understand the material. A learning circle could help - I was thinking of even getting a private tutor.
Hamish	Private tutors can be expensive – you're welcome to join us and it won't cost you anything. Every week we're going to begin the session with problems and questions from material that we've been given in the lecture. We want the learning circle to be practical and worthwhile, so that we all help each other to do well.
Anita	Do you think the others in the group would mind if I joined as well?
Hamish	Of course not – there are only five of us and you know us all.
Anita	I've been researching some past exam papers, so I'd be happy to contribute those to the circle if I join.
Hamish	One of the others suggested doing that too. He thought that we should try and identify any trends or common questions that were included in the past papers and that way we could prepare a little better for the final exam.
Anita	Yeah, that's what I was thinking. In fact, I've already started looking at last year's exams.
Hamish	Great – we're also going to hold mock tutorials, so we can practise our presentations on a smaller group before we have to do the real thing.
Anita	I am so worried about that. I'm dreading that first presentation – I've never done any kind of public speaking before.
Hamish	Well, you're not alone – I think we're all pretty nervous about it but we're hoping that the mocks will give us all a bit of confidence for the real tutorial. We don't want the group to be competitive – just collaborative – you know, working together and helping each other.
Anita	It sounds like you've really thought the learning circle idea through – you seem well-planned.
Hamish	It's just that when we all met last week to discuss the idea, we all had a list of objectives – you know, what we wanted to get out of a learning circle. That made the planning quite easy. Look, why don't you come next week to our first circle and you

	can see if it's what you're looking for. If not, well, you won't have lost anything and you can always organize a tutor for yourself afterwards.
Anita	Yeah, I think I will. When and where are you going to meet?
Hamish	Our inaugural meeting of the circle is on Thursday evening – from 6 to 8 in Ryan Hall.
Anita	OK – I'll be there.
Hamish	We plan to talk about any material that we've had trouble with from the lecture first and then, we thought we'd talk about our individual learning styles. Even though we all know each other as friends, we thought that because it'll be our first time together as a <u>study</u> group, it might be useful.
Anita	I'm not exactly sure what my learning style is!
Hamish	Give it some thought during the week and try to notice <u>how</u> you study – some people summarise everything or re-write lecture notes every week – others like to highlight the important points or group similar bits of information together. People like me – well, I have to read material at least three times before I can really comprehend it.
Anita	Really? I'm a writer I guess – I have to write everything down or I forget it straight away! I use the computer a lot.
Hamish	See – you <u>do</u> know how you learn – you just had to think about it.
Anita	I'll bring the exam papers and the research that I've started.
Hamish	We probably won't have time to look through them at our first meeting.
Anita	I'll bring them anyway – just in case. I think this learning circle idea is going to be a great success!

That is the end of Section 3. You now have ½ minute to check your answers.

Now turn to Section 4 of your Listening Question Booklet.

SECTION 4

You will hear a guest speaker at an Alternative Energy Seminar talking about wind-power.

First, look at Questions 31 to 40.

[SHORT PAUSE]

Now listen to the talk and answer Questions 31 to 40.

SPEAKER:

Good morning – thank you for giving me the opportunity to speak at this year's alternative energy seminar.

Right. Well – I know that the next speaker, John Dunkett, is going to talk about the mechanics of generating power using wind as an alternative source of energy, so I won't be using any technical terms and I won't be going into the technology of how wind generators actually work. I'll be concentrating on sharing my own experiences with you. For those of you who don't know, I live on a very windy farm some 3000 kilometres from the nearest city. That means we are not connected to the State Electricity Commission's grid and we have to produce our own electricity. When I first bought the farm in 1975, we got our electricity supply exclusively from diesel and petrol generators. The problems with this were two-fold: a lot of fuel was wasted because the generators usually didn't run to their full capacity and more importantly to my wife, the generators were extremely noisy – especially at night.

After we'd been on the farm for about six months, I heard about what they called a Hybrid System. This meant that we could keep the diesel generator but we also got a generator that was powered by wind. Because our place is so consistently windy – especially in summer – our hybrid system worked very well. In fact, we couldn't believe how well it worked!

We also had friends closer to the city who bought this hybrid system at the same time, and they were very pleased with the efficiency of it as well. Their farm is considerably less windy than ours – so even in moderately windy sites, the hybrid system appeared to work well.

Both of us agreed that we made substantial savings in fuel at the end of the first year and of course, our wives were happier – because it wasn't as noisy, as often!

In 1984, we found that we were rarely using our diesel generator and decided to try our hand at becoming self-sufficient in wind-generated power. We were sure that we'd survive without the back-up of the diesel generator, so we imported four wind generators from Denmark. America and Australia were dabbling in the technology, but we were too far behind the Europeans. The benefits of wind generators were much more obvious to the Danes and now as a result, they supply about 50% of wind turbines around the world.

Anyway, the Danish wind generators had a rated power output of 55 kilowatts per generator. They made quite an impact on our landscape and even though we could sometimes hear the mechanical noise from the generator itself, they were very quiet. The rotor diameters were about 20 metres. We felt proud that we were only using energy from clear, moving air to generate our electricity – no diesel or petrol or fuel smells either! We knew that our resource was renewable – we are after all, not going to run out of wind, especially at our place. The wind turbine is used to charge-up batteries which store the energy.

Last year, we bought a 600-kilowatt machine – it is about 46 metres high with a rotor-diameter of 43.5 metres. We found that the cost of the turbine was recovered within about 8 months. It should produce over 1,000,000 kilowatt hours per year for us. It does look a bit strange against our flat terrain but we love it. Best of all, my wife says she can't even hear the "windmill" as she calls it, from our house at night. Frankly, I think her hearing just isn't what it used to be – but I must agree that it is very quiet. Additionally, we expect it to last for about 20 years with regular six-monthly maintenance.

Our farm is isolated and yet, you'd be amazed by the number of visitors we have each year to inspect our wind turbines and the effectiveness of the wind generators. Actually, we often joke that when we stop making money from the farm, we'll charge tourists to come and visit our very own wind-farm. There is also the possibility of selling the electricity that we generate back to the Electricity Commission but I think that is all in the future. We've had a lot of people ask us why we chose wind-power generated energy rather than solar energy but as soon as they visit our windy farm, they know why. Even if our farm were not as windy as it is, we'd make that choice again. From all accounts, it is the least expensive form of renewable energy technology that we have. It can be used in a variety of applications from isolated farms such as ours, to supplying small sailboats without power.

Now, I'll hand you over to John Dunkett from the Danish company that sold us our original four wind turbines and he'll explain how this remarkable technology has developed over the last 20 or 30 years.

That is the end of Section 4 and the end of the Listening Test. You now have ½ minute to check your answers.

[PAUSE]

You now have 10 minutes to transfer your answers to your Answer Booklet.

SCORE ANALYSER – READING & LISTENING

After completing each of the *404 Essential Tests for IELTS* practice tests, use the Score Analyser to see
    a.   if your results are higher in the earlier sections than the later sections of the tests, or
    b.   if your errors are made in certain question types.

Follow the three steps outlined below to analyse your errors.

Step 1   Firstly, record your result for each section in the reading and listening tests.

TEST 1

TEST 1	Listening		
Section	Questions	Total	Your Score
1	1 – 10	10	
2	11 – 20	10	
3	21 – 30	10	
4	31 – 40	10	
		40	

TEST 1	Reading		
Passage	Questions	Total	Your Score
1	1 – 6	6	
1	7 – 12	6	
1	13 – 18	6	
2	19 – 24	6	
2	25 – 30	6	
3	31 – 40	10	
		40	

TEST 2

TEST 2	Listening		
Section	Questions	Total	Your Score
1	1 – 10	10	
2	11 – 20	10	
3	21 – 30	10	
4	31 – 40	10	
		40	

TEST 2	Reading		
Passage	Questions	Total	Your Score
1	1 – 6	6	
1	7 – 13	7	
2	14 – 20	7	
2	21 – 27	7	
3	28 – 40	13	
		40	

TEST 3

TEST 3	Listening		
Section	Questions	Total	Your Score
1	1 – 10	10	
2	11 – 20	10	
3	21 – 30	10	
4	31 – 40	10	
		40	

TEST 3	Reading		
Passage	Questions	Total	Your Score
1	1 – 6	6	
1	7 – 13	7	
2	14 – 21	8	
2	22 – 27	6	
3	28 – 40	13	
		40	

TEST 4

TEST 4	Listening		
Section	Questions	Total	Your Score
1	1 – 10	10	
2	11 – 20	10	
3	21 – 30	10	
4	31 – 40	10	
		40	

TEST 4	Reading		
Passage	Questions	Total	Your Score
1	1 – 6	6	
1	7 – 13	7	
2	14 – 20	7	
2	21 – 27	7	
3	28 – 40	13	
		40	

SCORE ANALYSER – READING & LISTENING continued

Step 2 Secondly, write the number of incorrect answers you made in each of the question sets below.

Then, note the question type in which your incorrect answers occur.

Use this to study whether or not there is a pattern to your mistakes and give yourself opportunities to practise the question types that you find difficult.

TEST 1

TEST 1	Listening		
Question Types	Question Sets	Total	Total incorrect
Completing sentences	5 – 10 31 – 32 37 – 40	12	
Completing tables	11 – 16 27 – 30 33 – 36	14	
Labelling	17 – 20	4	
Multiple choice	21 – 22	2	
Multiple choice x 2	23 – 26	4	
Short-answer	1 – 4	4	
		40	

TEST 1	Reading		
Question Types	Question Sets	Total	Total incorrect
Completing tables	31 – 34	4	
Completing summaries	25 – 30	6	
Heading bank	1 – 6	6	
Matching	13 – 18	6	
Multiple choice	37 – 40	4	
Short-answer	7 – 12 35 – 36	8	
Identifying viewpoints, facts and opinions	19 – 24	6	
		40	

TEST 2

TEST 2	Listening		
Question Types	Question Sets	Total	Total incorrect
Completing sentences	16 – 20 26 – 30	10	
Completing summaries	31 – 34	4	
Completing forms & tables	1 – 5 6 – 10 35 – 39	15	
Multiple choice	11 – 13 21 – 25	8	
Multiple choice x 2	14 – 15	2	
Short-answer	40	1	
		40	

TEST 2	Reading		
Question Types	Question Sets	Total	Total incorrect
Completing sentences	21 – 27	7	
Completing summaries	32 – 35	4	
Labelling	1 – 3	3	
Matching	7 – 13 28 – 31 36 – 40	16	
Multiple choice	4 – 6	3	
Identifying viewpoints, facts and opinions	14 – 20	7	
		40	

Step 2   continued

TEST 3

TEST 3	Listening		
Question Types	Question Sets	Total	Total incorrect
Completing sentences	6 – 7 25 – 30 31 – 32 40	11	
Completing tables	8 – 10 14 – 20 22 – 24 37 – 39	16	
Labelling	3 – 5	3	
Multiple choice	1 – 2 11 – 13 21	6	
Multiple choice x 2	33 – 36	4	
		40	

TEST 3	Reading		
Question Types	Question Sets	Total	Total incorrect
Completing sentences	14 – 21	8	
Completing summaries	34 – 40	7	
Heading bank	22 – 27	6	
Short-answer	7 – 13	7	
Identifying viewpoints, facts and opinions	1 – 6 28 – 33	12	
		40	

TEST 4

TEST 4	Listening		
Question Types	Question Sets	Total	Total incorrect
Completing sentences	10 31 – 32 40	4	
Completing summaries	17 – 20	4	
Completing forms & tables	11 – 16 33 – 36 37 – 39	13	
Labelling	5 – 9	5	
Matching	21 – 24	4	
Multiple choice	1 – 4 25 – 27 28	8	
Multiple choice x 2	29 – 30	2	
		40	

TEST 4	Reading		
Question Types	Question Sets	Total	Total incorrect
Completing tables	33 – 38	6	
Completing sentences	14 – 20	7	
Labelling	9 – 13	5	
Multiple choice	7 – 8 39 – 40	5	
Matching	21 – 27	7	
Short-answer	1 – 6	6	
Identifying viewpoints, facts and opinions	28 – 32	5	
		40	

☞ Your results should be higher in the earlier sections of the tests than the later sections of the tests.

SCORE ANALYSER – READING & LISTENING continued

Step 3   **Thirdly, check your scores on the Score Interpreter below.** This will give you a good idea of the level of English you are currently at, and whether you will need additional English study before taking the IELTS test or applying to the Immigration Department of the country you wish to live, work or study in.

When looking at your results, don't worry too much if you don't improve with every practice test. There may be some tests, and some sections, that you will find easier than others due to your English vocabulary or your knowledge/understanding of the subject.

Remember that this Score Interpreter should be used as a guide for your reading and listening ability only. It was compiled after thorough analysis of the trial results undertaken with the *404 Essential Tests for IELTS*. It provides a good indication of your ability and potential to do well, but remember that a good score there is no guarantee of a good score in the actual IELTS test.

Score Interpreter

No. of correct answers	Implications
0 – 7	You will need at least 30 weeks of intensive, formal, full-time English study before attempting the IELTS test. A score like this indicates that you need to improve your knowledge of English vocabulary, your reading speed in English and your listening. Moreover, it is very likely that your other skills will also need much improvement. Don't attempt any more practice tests until you have done some more English study. Read the advice in *101 Helpful Hints for IELTS*.
8 – 15	You will need at least 20 weeks of intensive, formal, full-time English study before attempting the IELTS test. There is much you can do to help improve your English. Use the Score Analyser to discover if your difficulties result from a specific or systematic problem, or the time restrictions. By targeting your problem areas, you can focus on improvement. Try some other reading practice before taking the next practice test. Complete the exercises in *202 Useful Exercises for IELTS*.
16 – 23	You will need to study for at least another 10 weeks of intensive English before taking the IELTS test. Increase your exposure to other reading texts and listen more to English being spoken. Do not just complete the practice tests. Also see the suggestions made in the Introduction to *404 Essential Tests for IELTS* – in particular, try the Immersion Ideas that are outlined.
24 – 28	This score indicates a good level of English. It should be sufficient to gain acceptance into high school – if that is your aim. It may also be enough for immigration to some English-speaking countries.
29 – 34	This is a very good score and it should be good enough for you to gain acceptance into most countries for work, dependent upon the requirements of the job you are hoping to do. If you are getting these scores in this area for all of the tests in this book, then you are more than ready to attempt the IELTS test.
35 – 40	Well done! This score shows that you have an excellent knowledge of English. If your score in reading and listening can be matched in the speaking and writing sections of the IELTS test, you would be more than able to cope with working, living or studying in an English-speaking country. Pack your bags!

 Always check with the particular country you wish to apply to, as entry requirements vary.

IELTS LISTENING TEST ANSWER SHEET

Question Number: Answer:

Name: ....

Question Number	Answer				Question Number	Answer		
1		▭ 1 ▭			22		▭ 22 ▭	
2		▭ 2 ▭			23		▭ 23 ▭	
3		▭ 3 ▭			24		▭ 24 ▭	
4		▭ 4 ▭			25		▭ 25 ▭	
5		▭ 5 ▭			26		▭ 26 ▭	
6		▭ 6 ▭			27		▭ 27 ▭	
7		▭ 7 ▭			28		▭ 28 ▭	
8		▭ 8 ▭			29		▭ 29 ▭	
9		▭ 9 ▭			30		▭ 30 ▭	
10		▭ 10 ▭			31		▭ 31 ▭	
11		▭ 11 ▭			32		▭ 32 ▭	
12		▭ 12 ▭			33		▭ 33 ▭	
13		▭ 13 ▭			34		▭ 34 ▭	
14		▭ 14 ▭			35		▭ 35 ▭	
15		▭ 15 ▭			36		▭ 36 ▭	
16		▭ 16 ▭			37		▭ 37 ▭	
17		▭ 17 ▭			38		▭ 38 ▭	
18		▭ 18 ▭			39		▭ 39 ▭	
19		▭ 19 ▭			40		▭ 40 ▭	
20		▭ 20 ▭						
21		▭ 21 ▭						

Listening Total:

Band Score

Marker's Initials

~ For use with the 404 Essential Tests for IELTS ~

IELTS READING TEST ANSWER SHEET

Question
Number: Answer:

Name: ....

Question Number	Answer			Question Number	Answer		
1		1		22		22	
2		2		23		23	
3		3		24		24	
4		4		25		25	
5		5		26		26	
6		6		27		27	
7		7		28		28	
8		8		29		29	
9		9		30		30	
10		10		31		31	
11		11		32		32	
12		12		33		33	
13		13		34		34	
14		14		35		35	
15		15		36		36	
16		16		37		37	
17		17		38		38	
18		18		39		39	
19		19		40		40	
20		20					
21		21					

Reading Total:	
Band Score	
Marker's Initials	

~ For use with the 404 Essential Tests for IELTS ~

IELTS WRITING TEST 1 2 3 4 **ANSWER SHEET**

Name: ....

....

....

....

....

....

....

....

....

....

....

....

....

....

....

....

....

....

....

....

....

....

....

....

~ For use with the 404 Essential Tests for IELTS ~

··

··

··

··

··

··

··

··

··

··

··

··

··

··

··

··

··

··

··

··

··

~ *For use with the 404 Essential Tests for IELTS* ~

GLOSSARY OF TERMS

Check the meaning and spelling of the following words and phrases in a good English dictionary...

(The terms are not specific to one test. To avoid repetition they are listed where they first occur.)

...IN ESSENTIAL PRACTICE TEST 1

aspiring	....
adjustable	....
vintage	....
circa	....
extension	....
fluorescent tubes	....
antiques	....
campuses	....
cosmopolitan	....
disaster	....
queries	....
motivate	....
appliances	....
instructional	....
ever-changing	....
documentary	....
mandatory	....
volunteer	....
undertake	....
exemption	....
threshold	....
alternative	....
initial	....
flexible	....
key (v)	....
benchmark (n)	....
implement	....
provisions	....
pose a risk	....
inseparable	....
overcome	....
monument	....
ensuing	....
reveal	....
cynics	....
gender	....
....	....

...IN ESSENTIAL PRACTICE TEST 2

implies	incidence
enclosed	....
comparable	....
versatile	....
deterred	....
collapses	....
series	....
sloping	....
ramps	....
seclusion	....
illuminated	....
options	....
themes	....
appointment	....
souvenir	....
prior	....
mediate	....
arbitrate	....
expiry	....
dynamic	....
recruit	....
candidate	....
unique	....
withdraw	....
potential	....
role play	....
adolescents	....
attributes	....
vigilant	....
infections	....
potentially	....
trigger (v)	....
overwhelming	....
reiterates	....
respiratory	....
in conjunction with	....
symptoms	....

GLOSSARY OF TERMS continued

...IN ESSENTIAL PRACTICE TEST 3

hazards	lucrative
occurrence	undoubtedly
installation	modification
maintenance	crop
recreational	....
like-minded	....
to gear up for	....
litter	....
inclusive	....
admission	....
spectator	....
dedicated	....
concept	....
recycle	....
thorough	....
keen	....
participate	....
consult	....
motivate	....
impact (n)	....
eligible	....
initiative	....
insight	....
sustainable	....
ongoing	....
potential	....
host (adj)	....
assess	....
recipient	....
ethical	....
altering	....
consumed	....
dispute	....
undue	....
strict	....
hesitate	....
banned	....
proponents	....
malnutrition	....

...IN ESSENTIAL PRACTICE TEST 4

nourish	....
to guard against	....
manually	....
patented	....
array	....
contend	....
receipt	....
warranty	....
parts (n)	....
delay (v)	....
timesheet	....
bill (v)	....
client	....
incur	....
optional	....
decline	....
productivity	....
workshop (n)	....
seminar	....
worthwhile	....
morale	....
contented	....
quitting	....
rapidly	....
worn-out	....
diet (n)	....
abnormal	....
exposure	....
inhaled	....
lodge	....
diagnose	....
localised	....
persistent	....
hereditary	....
behavioural	....
....	....
....	....
....	....
....	....

GLOSSARY OF TERMS continued

alternative	cloze	expertise	immerse	operational	requirement
analyse	compare	extent	inference	paraphrase	scan
appropriate	compensate	factor	interaction	partial	singular
assess	competence	familiarise	interchangeable	peer	skim
breakdown	context	fluent	interview *(n)*	plural	summary
candidate	contraction	focus	label *(v)*	precede	synonym
category	describe	gap	logical	prepare	systematic
characteristic	dialogue	glance	match	proficiency	task
circle *(v)*	discuss	headings	monologue	prompt *(n)*	transfer
circumstances	double-check	highlight	non-tertiary	provide	valid
classify	evaluate	identify	occasional	report	vocabulary

Table of words often used in instructions in the IELTS examinations and in explanatory guides such as the Introduction section of this book and the *Study Guides to the 404 Essential Tests for IELTS*.

Sentence Completion Exercise:

Complete the sentences below using the words in the table above. The answers are given on page 84.

1. Potential university students must sit for the IELTS Academic Module but applicants for high schools, technical colleges or other .... institutions can sit for the General Training Module.

2. The listening and reading sections of the IELTS test use synonyms and words with similar meanings for key words in the questions. Candidates with a wide range of .... will find it easier to locate the answers.

3. An important writing skill is being able to express an opinion and give clear, ... examples. These can be from personal experience but they must be related to the topic.

4. As well as completing the practice tests in this book, you should try to read widely in order to .... yourself for the test and improve your vocabulary.

5. Speaking English at every opportunity and practising the speaking .... in *404 Essential Tests for IELTS* with peers or teachers can greatly increase a candidate's confidence.

6. When preparing for the speaking section of the IELTS test, you should always make sure that you .... on extending and improving your knowledge and use of grammar.

7. After completing the practice tests, you should .... your answers and try to identify the kinds of errors that you made.

8. Results from an IELTS test are generally accepted by institutions for a period of two years after taking the test. After that, they are no longer .... and you will need to sit for the test again.

· 125 ·

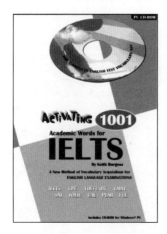

101 Helpful Hints for IELTS is actually two books – one for each IELTS Module – Academic or General Training. Both include two practice Listening and Speaking Tests, four Reading and Writing Tests, and an extensive Help Section, covering all four sub-tests of the IELTS examination. The unique format of the books enables students to complete the first practice test and review their performance before attempting the next test. This is achieved by linking each hint to the appropriate pages of each test, so that students can identify problem areas and understand why they may have made errors. The tests increase in difficulty as students progress through the book. **101 Helpful Hints for IELTS** are comprehensive course books for use in the classroom or self-study.

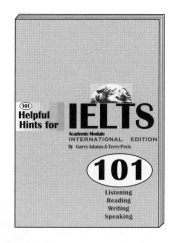

Audio CD

Cassette

Book

101 Helpful Hints for IELTS
Academic Module   International Edition

Book:	ISBN 978-0-9587604-6-1
Cassette:	ISBN 978-0-9578980-0-4*
Book & Audio CDs(2):	ISBN 978-0-9578980-6-6

101 Helpful Hints for IELTS
General Training Module   International Edition

Book:	ISBN 978-0-9587604-9-2
Cassette:	ISBN 978-0-9578980-0-4*
Book & Audio CDs(2):	ISBN 978-0-9578980-9-7

*the listening test is the same for both Modules of the test

Audio CDs

Cassette

Book

202 Useful Exercises for IELTS is our IELTS practice workbook, designed to give students of English extensive and guided IELTS examination practice. It is also a very effective learning aid for migrants and students taking EFL Secondary School Preparation Courses.

The book is divided into 5 sections, each focussing on a topic relevant to the examination, and contains:

- *27 listening exercises* – 8 news items, 5 academic lectures and 3 dictations, (all with complete tapescripts)
- *5 reading passages* – with gapfill exercises, short-answer questions, sentence completion tasks, multiple choice, True/False style questions and matching tasks
- *10 writing tasks* – with complete Model Answers.

The 202 exercises complement the advice given in **101 Helpful Hints for IELTS**. Also included are punctuation, spelling, grammar and vocabulary exercises. A complete Answer Key for all exercises and a comprehensive index are provided for reference.

202 Useful Exercises for IELTS
Academic/General   International Edition

Book:	ISBN 978-0-9587604-7-8
Cassette:	ISBN 978-0-9578980-1-1
Book & Audio CDs(2):	ISBN 978-0-9578980-7-3

202 Useful Exercises for IELTS
Academic/General   Australasian Edition

Book:	ISBN 978-0-9587604-5-4
Cassette:	ISBN 978-0-9578980-2-8
Book & Audio CDs(2):	ISBN 978-0-9578980-5-9

404 Essential Tests for IELTS – Academic Module includes four complete practice tests for the Academic version of the IELTS examination. It has been written to give candidates extensive practice with instructions, question types and content used in the actual IELTS tests and includes detailed descriptions of the four test sections.

Audio CDs

Cassettes

Book

404 Essential Tests for IELTS
Academic Module   International Edition

Book:	ISBN 978-0-9751832-0-5
Cassettes(2):	ISBN 978-0-9751832-1-2
Book & Audio CDs(2):	ISBN 978-0-9751832-2-9

speaking writing reading

advice video clips quizzes

tips audio exercises
games tests

Visit our website at

http://www.aapress.com.au

and

help yourself to

FREE *IELTS PRACTICE EXERCISES*

TO **DOWNLOAD NOW**

AND MUCH MORE...

study tips

study links

forums

chat room

test your English

FAQ

'how much do you know' quiz

web polls

etc.

NEW

IELTS
101 **ONLINE COURSE**
1-3 MONTHS STUDY

DETAILS AT
http://aapress.com.au/ielts101